Catherine the Great

and the

Enlightenment

in Russia

Catherine the Great and the Enlightenment in Russia

Nancy Whitelaw

MORGAN REYNOLDS
Publishing, Inc.

620 South Elm Street, Suite 223
Greensboro, North Carolina 27406
http://www.morganreynolds.com

European Queens

Queen Isabella
Catherine de' Medici
Catherine the Great
Marie Antoinette
Queen Victoria

CATHERINE THE GREAT AND THE ENLIGHTENMENT IN RUSSIA

Library of Congress Cataloging-in-Publication Data

Whitelaw, Nancy.
    Catherine the Great and the Enlightenment in Russia / Nancy Whitelaw.
        p. cm. — (European queens)
    Includes bibliographical references and index.
    ISBN 1-931798-27-3 (library binding)
    1. Catherine II, Empress of Russia, 1729-1796—Juvenile literature. 2.
Empresses—Russia—Biography—Juvenile literature. 3.
Russia—History—Catherine II, 1762-1796—Juvenile literature. I. Title.
II. Series.
    DK170.W48 2004
    947'.063'092—dc22

                            2004014711

Printed in the United States of America
First Edition

Dedicated to Bob and Dee Keller with many thanks and much love for your help and friendship

Contents

Catherine the Great of Russia *(Courtesy of Art Resource.)*

1

A German Princess

On June 28, 1744 Sophia Augusta Frederica approached the altar hand-in-hand with the Czarina Elizabeth. The current and future rulers of Russia wore beautiful and elaborate matching gowns of dark red threaded with silver. Sophia, a slim, attractive girl of fifteen, had recently been ill and was still wan and pale. Elizabeth, by contrast, was an imposing figure—a large woman, radiantly healthy, draped in jewels. As Czarina Elizabeth's court looked on, the priest of the Orthodox Church began the long ceremony that would finalize Sophie's conversion from the Lutheran faith to the Russian Orthodox religion. The sweet smell of incense hung heavily in the richly ornate church as Sophie read the fifty pages of her script with poise and confidence. She had only been studying Russian for a few months, but she had worked hard and it showed. When it came time for

Prince Christian Augustus of Anhalt-Zerbst.

her to recite the creed of the Orthodox Church, she did so flawlessly and without hesitation.

Elizabeth was moved to tears as the young princess was officially baptized into her new faith and given the new name Catherine Alexeyevna. Immediately after the ceremony she presented Catherine with a priceless diamond necklace and matching brooch. Catherine offered her thanks and retired to her room. Though celebrations would last far into the night, she needed to rest. She was still weak and on the next day she would be officially engaged to her future husband and become the Grand Duchess of Russia.

The next seventeen years would test all of Catherine's cunning, fortitude, and intelligence. By marrying the heir to the Russian throne, she entered perhaps the most ruthless court in Europe. Despised by her husband and for many years detested by the Russian people, who saw her as a German interloper into Russian affairs, the fact she survived is remarkable. That she became one of the most powerful rulers of the eighteenth century is almost miraculous.

The princess who became Catherine the Great of Russia was born Sophia Augusta Frederica Anhalt-Zerbst on April 21, 1729. She was the daughter of Christian Augustus and Johanna Elizabeth, minor members of the Anhalt-Zerbst noble family. Christian was a prince, but a poor

Johanna Elizabeth of Holstein-Gottorp.

and obscure prince among many Germans with the same title. Johanna Elizabeth was a once beautiful and ambitious woman who had grown bitter that a better marriage had not been arranged for her.

As a small child, Sophie did not show much promise of developing into a beauty like her mother. Disappointed, Johanna pushed the young girl away. Sophie's father loved her but had little time to spend with her. When she was four years old, Sophie was taken to an official reception in honor of King Frederick William I of Prussia. Told to kiss the hem of the short robe he was wearing, Sophie refused, saying that it was too high for her to reach. The court laughed, but Johanna was horrified by her daughter's outspoken obstinacy and set out to teach her how to properly humble herself.

She wanted to make the best possible marriage for her daughter as a way to elevate her own status, and feared no one would want a stubborn, willful bride. It was not as though she was so beautiful, Johanna pointed out, that a wealthy prince would tolerate her disobedience. Sophie did learn excellent manners, but she always believed that her mother was teaching her to be deceitful and to hide her true thoughts.

Though the family was not wealthy, Johanna spent extravagantly on tutors and dancing teachers for Sophie and her younger brother. Sophie attended balls and banquets dressed like a tiny adult in corsets, low-cut dresses, and with powdered hair. She learned the protocols of court life—how to curtsey, the proper way to say hello and good-bye, and how to kiss the hems of the dresses or robes of the ladies and lords. Constantly reminded by her mother that she was not a pretty child, she learned to use her wits to charm adults.

A French governess, Babet Cardel, was her favorite tutor. Cardel was intelligent and kindly; she cared for Sophie deeply. She read classic French literature with her and Sophie soon became skilled in the French language. She plowed through the works of most of the well known writers of the day—plays by Racine and Molière, poems and stories by La Fontaine. French was the language of diplomacy, spoken in all the courts of Europe and by the aristocracy throughout the continent. It was necessary that Sophie learn to speak it as though it was her first language.

Sophie received the thorough religious instruction customary to young people of her social rank. Her natural curiosity got her into some trouble with her Lutheran pastor, however, when she asked several impertinent questions about the infinite goodness of God, the truth of the scriptures, and the Last Judgement. Only Babet's intervention kept Sophie from being whipped

Princess Sophia Augusta Frederica of Anhalt-Zerbst in 1740. *(Courtesy of the Staaliche Bildstelle.)*

for her refusal to accept without question what she was told. Though the young girl was devout, she was also a thinker. Sophie also had a terrible time with music classes. She had no appreciation for either tunes or rhythms. She later admitted, "Rarely is music anything but noise to my ears."

Sophie was most happy playing games with other children from the court. Sometimes middle class children would be allowed to come to the palace and play. Their games were usually rough and boisterous—too much so for her mother's taste. Sophie loved to be in charge, and though some of her playmates said she was bossy, there was no doubt she was a natural leader.

Happily, and contrary to her mother's expectations, Sophie's appearance improved as she aged. By thirteen, she was an attractive young girl, slim and well proportioned, with brilliant blue-black eyes and thick chestnut-colored hair. Her chin was still too sharp, but her intelligence radiated from her so strongly many found it difficult to remember her physical features after meeting her. She was clearly a force of nature. But she still fretted about her looks. Despite the improvements in the face she saw in the mirror, she was never able to believe she was pretty. The most she could hope was that she need not be ashamed of her looks. She told her journal that though she was not beautiful, she knew how to please people with her conversation and charm. Johanna only hoped her daughter would be able to make a good marriage.

Frederick II of Prussia, who had succeeded his father Frederick William I, used betrothals so assiduously that he became known as the matchmaker of Europe. He created several powerful alliances through arranged marriages. He took advantage of the fact Prussia was the most powerful of all the German states and of the simple fact that children of nobility could only marry other children of the nobility, which meant there was always a limited number of eligible candidates for any prince or princess in need of a mate. Needless to say, marriages were not about love; they were all politics. A good marriage strengthened the relationship between two countries and their ruling families.

Ivan Antonovich (Ivan VI), as portrayed by I. Leopold, in 1741 during his brief reign under his mother's regency before being overthrown and imprisoned by Elizabeth.

Czarina Elizabeth I of Russia was the daughter of Peter the Great, who had tried, usually against its will, to drag Russia into the modern world. Elizabeth had been engaged to Sophie's uncle, her mother's brother, but he had died of smallpox before the wedding. Elizabeth had, apparently, actually loved her fiancé and after his death she refused to even consider marrying anyone else.

Elizabeth was a powerful ruler who had taken the throne by force by deposing two-year-old Ivan VI, and his mother,

Czarina Elizabeth. *(The Hermitage Museum, St. Petersburg, Russia.)*

the Regent Anna Leopoldovna. Worried that Anna was planning to have her arrested to keep her from the throne, Elizabeth had decided to act first. She put on the uniform of her troops, mounted a horse, and led her army into the capital where she ordered both the baby Ivan and his mother imprisoned. It was an illegal seizure of power but no one dared to challenge the daughter of Peter the Great. She had commanded the huge Russian kingdom with authority and fearsome certainty ever since.

Soon after she took the throne, Elizabeth began looking for an heir. As long as Ivan VI was alive, there was a possibility that his supporters among the nobility would try to overthrow her and bring him to power. Elizabeth needed to have an heir lined up to discourage conspiracies. She plucked another nephew, young Peter Feodorovich, the son of her deceased older sister, from Germany. Elizabeth brought him to Russia and raised Peter as her own. But he was a great disappointment. Peter turned out to be weak, vain, and foolish. He cared nothing for books or politics and preferred to spend his time riding his horse in a Prussian military uniform and playing endlessly with his toy soldiers. When the time came to secure him a bride, Elizabeth knew she needed to find a brave young woman who could compensate for Peter's many inadequacies. She asked Emperor Frederick II of Prussia for advice.

Though Peter was not attractive or smart, he was a highly sought-after prize. Any girl who married him could—if she had the wit and strength to survive the dangerous Russian court—one day become czarina of all Russia. Kings, princes, dukes, and all manner of nobility from all over Europe schemed to have their daughters, nieces, cousins, and sisters considered. Of all the available candidates, Frederick II recommended the young German princess Sophie of Anhalt-Zerbst as the best choice to be Peter's bride.

Elizabeth pondered Frederick's suggestion. She knew he was not only thinking about the good of Russia when he made the recommendation. Frederick wanted to strengthen the ties between Russia and Prussia. Finally, Elizabeth decided that it would be a good match. Because she had been engaged to Sophie's uncle she knew the family well. Also, Sophie and Peter were cousins, which was considered to be a benefit. There was no taboo against cousin marriage; rather, it was a way to make family ties stronger. Elizabeth decided to see the girl before making a final decision. It was important to keep the process secret to avoid setting off a conflict between competing families and to stave off any Russians who would be opposed to the possibility of having yet another German czarina. Elizabeth sent Johanna a secret message inviting her and Sophie to Moscow.

When she received the letter, Johanna could hardly believe the good news. Her stubborn daughter might make her a rich and powerful woman. Sophie's father was not as happy. He was deeply religious and knew that Sophie would have to renounce his Lutheran faith and accept the teachings of the Russian Orthodox Church—but the choice was not his to make. After countless arguments over what to take, Sophie packed up her meager wardrobe and few possessions and traveled with her mother to St. Petersburg. She would never see her father, her beloved governess, or her childhood home again.

The first stop on their journey was Emperor Frederick II's palace in Berlin. He wanted to examine the girl he was sending to Elizabeth. It was important that she not be a disappointment. He was dismayed when Johanna politely told him Sophie was too ill to be seen. For three days, the emperor waited. His patience ran out and he demanded to see the princess. Johanna had no choice but to reveal the truth—Sophie could not present herself to him because she had nothing appropriate to wear and no money to buy a dress. Frederick immediately sent her a dress that belonged to one of his sisters and fourteen-year-old Sophie was brought before him that very night.

The story of the poor princess with no wardrobe spread quickly through the court. Everyone was eager to see how she would conduct herself before the emperor in her borrowed finery. The room was full of tension when Sophie was seated next to Frederick at dinner. Although she was shy at first, she soon opened up to Frederick's gentle and kind conversation. Her manners were without fault, and her intelligence, wit, and good humor impressed the emperor. When Sophie left he was confident that he had made a good choice.

Once they crossed the border into Russia, Elizabeth provided money and transportation for the rest of their journey. Sophie and her mother traveled to St. Petersburg in a sleigh drawn by twelve horses. Sophie had never seen such a splendid sleigh. It had scarlet draperies decorated with silver braid and a feather bed with covers of satin and precious fur. Heading east, they happened to pass several black sleighs under heavy guard going the other direction. When Sophie asked whom those carriages might contain, her respondent paled, then changed the subject. Sophie would eventually learn that Ivan VI and his mother were the mysterious passengers and that they were on their way to the fortress where Elizabeth had imprisoned them. Had she known that at the time, her own journey might not have seemed so exciting.

After a month of travel that, even in their luxurious sleigh, was bone jarring, the little caravan reached St. Petersburg, the westward facing city that Peter the Great had chosen for his capital. They stayed long enough to equip Sophie with more lavish dresses than she had ever dreamed of owning. Sophie was shown the road Elizabeth, dressed in her military uniform, had ridden down the day she seized the throne of Russia. The young princess was captivated by the story and the image of a brave and proud czarina astride a horse at the head of her army.

A portrait by Georg Cristoph Grooth of Czarina Elizabeth in military dress, much as she was described to Princess Sophie. *(The Tretyakov Gallery, Moscow, Russia.)*

Johanna's connections at court had suggested it would make a favorable impression on Elizabeth if they arrived in time for the first night of the Grand Duke Peter's birthday celebration. There was no time to linger. They completed the four-hundred-mile trip to Moscow in just four days, passing through the city gates early in the evening of February 9th. Moscow was a study in contrasts—a hundred splendid churches with gilded domes sat alongside wretched hovels. Ragged beggars rushed off the muddy streets to avoid being run over by the fancy carriages transporting men in powdered wigs and ladies in lavish and elegant clothes.

Sophie's first meeting with Peter, whom she had not seen

Peasants and merchants and carriages fill Moscow's elegant main square.

in years, was a tremendous disappointment. Though she had been warned that he was not particularly handsome or charming, nothing prepared her for the coarse and grinning imbecile before her. Elizabeth, on the other hand, was everything she had imagined. Sophie raved about her: "No one could see Elizabeth for the first time without being overwhelmed by her beauty and majesty. She was very tall and very stout, without it being in the least bit disfiguring…" Elizabeth, in turn, was moved by Johanna's resemblance to her dead fiancé and by young Sophie's grace and intelligence.

As Sophie would learn, Elizabeth, much like the city of Moscow, had many different faces. She was a devout parishioner of the Russian Orthodox Church who attended mass frequently, observed fasts, and venerated icons and relics. In her personal life, however, she took many lovers; there was even a persistent rumor that she had once married a Ukrainian peasant. She could be highly emotional and was extremely vain. She never wore the same dress twice and sometimes changed her clothes as often as three times a day.

She was said to have over fifteen thousand dresses. She controlled Russia absolutely, governing with authority and assurance. Her subjects were devoted to her, and she loved her country more than anything else. Sophie considered this to be her most impressive trait.

Compared to their life in Germany, Moscow was like a dream to Johanna and Sophie. They had servants at their beck and call and dinners and banquets fashioned for their pleasure. As Sophie and Peter got to know each other better, she confirmed her first impression that her future husband was an uneducated lout. Peter's mother, Elizabeth's older sister, had died when he was three months old and his father, a duke in the German state of Holstein, took little interest in his son. He died when Peter was eleven, and the young orphan was sent away to be educated with other German princes. The schedule of intensive study, strict discipline, and military drill had been difficult for Peter, who was physically weak, emotionally unbalanced, and not very intelligent. Over time he grew to love military marches and parades, although he never mastered school.

Sophie knew she had no choice but to try to make the situation work. She decided to treat Peter as though he were her younger brother. She was patient and kind with him and participated in his boyish games without complaint. She had been a tomboy growing up and was used to rough play. She let herself be ordered around like a soldier and listened sympathetically when her future husband told her that he loved a young lady named Lopukhina and was sad because she had been sent away. Sophie swallowed her pride and remembered her ultimate goal. As she wrote in her memoirs, "I cared very little for the grand duke, but I cared a lot about becoming a Czarina."

Elizabeth provided Sophia three tutors to prepare her for her new life. She studied the dogma and ritual of the Orthodox religion, the Russian language,

The Grand Duke Peter Feodorovich. *(Tretyakov Gallery.)*

and mastered the Russian social dances. She worked hard, determined to become a perfect pupil and a Russian by force of will. Peter, on the other hand, made no secret of his distaste for all things Russian. Sophie saw how that hurt the czarina. Peter's longing for his German home would grow stronger over the years. Sophie knew her own devotion to Russia would contrast to her benefit with the czarina and the Russian people, who were already deeply jealous and anxious about the German influence at court. The princess stayed up late at night, shivering in the seemingly always-cold palace, studying vocabulary and the complicated Russian grammar. She practiced saying the words before a mirror to see how her mouth shaped around the sounds to better eliminate her German accent. Although she still struggled with rhythm, she even became an adequate dancer—with the help of a ballet master.

Sophie's religious instructor was Simon Todorski, an accomplished theologian who spoke perfect German and who had, in the past, guided several Lutheran princesses into Orthodoxism. He introduced the mysterious rites of the Orthodox Church, explained the reasons for the incense, jeweled icons, embroidered robes, and chanted liturgies. Aware that his young charge had reservations about leaving the religion of her home and family, he convinced her that the two faiths were actually quite similar. Sophie conveyed this claim to her father, hoping to reassure him that "there was no fundamental difference between the Orthodox and Lutheran faiths." Perhaps she believed this; perhaps she did not. But accepting Russia, Peter, and a new religion were all necessary to achieving her goal. Living in the aura of Czarina Elizabeth, Sophia watched and planned. One day she would rule Russia in her own right.

2

Marriage and a New Life

Sophia was treated like royalty in Moscow, but her place was not secure until she was married. Elizabeth was a capricious woman who could easily change her mind. Sophie concentrated on being pious, modest, and pleasing.

Then she became seriously ill with pneumonia. Normally illness was considered a sign of weakness and could have led to her being replaced. But when the rumors began to spread that Sophie had worn her health down with late night studying, she won the court's sympathy. Elizabeth nursed and comforted the young girl herself; she admitted that she had come to like her. Even when fighting for her life, Sophie made politically shrewd decisions. Johanna wanted to call in a Lutheran minister in case last rites were needed, but Sophie insisted on seeing her Orthodox religious instructor instead. This act particularly endeared her to Elizabeth. Sophie also used her time in bed to take note of her maid's gossip and began to understand the intrigue that pervaded the court. She learned that Elizabeth had many lovers as well as strong appetites for food and alcohol. She heard how favorites were dismissed in disgrace for minor offenses, and how Elizabeth despaired at the thought of Peter succeeding her to the throne. More than anything, she wanted Peter to father a child she could put in his place.

Sophie was well enough to appear in court in April on her fifteenth birthday. She looked thin and drawn: "I had become thin as a skeleton" she wrote later, "my face and features were drawn, my hair was falling out, and I was mortally pale. I appeared to myself ugly as a scarecrow." Though she earned the favor of the court, she was constantly on guard. Peter was growing jealous because Elizabeth held up Sophie as an example of how a young person should prepare for the throne.

Johanna, too, was jealous of Sophie. She resented the attention her daughter received and often behaved badly in an effort to attract notice. Peter and Johanna, two temperamental people, clashed one day when Peter accidentally upset Johanna's carriage. Johanna called him "an uneducated lout." Peter sneered at her, and Sophie had to intervene. She made the quick decision to side with Peter in the conflict. There was nothing to gain by supporting her mother. Johanna's antics strengthened Sophie's determination to make Russia her new home.

Finally, in July, Elizabeth decided Sophie was ready to officially be accepted into her new family. First came her public conversion and baptism. The next day Catherine Alexeyevna became the Grand Duchess of Russia when she was formally betrothed to Peter. Catherine's diary entry afterward revealed her feelings: "My heart boded no good. I was sustained by ambition alone. There was something within me which never allowed me to doubt for a single moment that I should one day succeed in becoming Czarina of Russia, in my own right." The ceremony lasted for four hours, during which the entire assembly remained standing as bearded priests in golden robes paid homage to the couple. After they exchanged rings, cannons boomed and all the bells of Moscow rang. The next day, Catherine received thirty thousand rubles for spending money, more jewels, and her own court of ladies-in-waiting. She immediately sent some of the money to her father. He had been hurt when he was not invited to the wedding. Elizabeth did not want him there to object to the Orthodox ceremony.

As the wedding preparations began, Peter spent most of his time drinking with his friends. Catherine continued to be kind to him, always conscious that she needed to please both Elizabeth and Peter. He came to trust and confide in her, telling her how much he despised Russia and how little he wanted to become czar of such a miserable country. Catherine did not reveal to him that her desires were just the opposite, or that she spent hours studying books on government and philosophy. She was especially interested in the work of François Voltaire and his writings that laid the foundation for the new emphasis on observation, reason, and logic. Now referred to as the Age of Enlightenment, this secular movement began in France. Enlightenment thinkers rebelled against superstition and unthinking adherence to tradition. They believed progress could be made and great things could be achieved if only people could control their emotions and view the world through collected reason. In order for this to be possible, a greater number of people needed to be educated. Rulers and other decision-makers had to be the first to adopt these ideas.

Catherine wanted to implement the ideas of Voltaire and other philosophers she read. Furthermore, Russia was not a backwater at all. Peter the Great, Elizabeth's father, had attempted to govern like an enlightened ruler. He spent a lifetime trying to pull Russia out of its isolation and slavish adoration of the old ways. He introduced western ideas into its politics and economy. He had encouraged Russians to study abroad and to bring back technological skills to Russia. Most importantly, under Peter church and state were separated—a key component of Enlightenment thinking. He even asked his subjects to wear western dress and to shave their long beards. Peter had not succeeded in fundamentally altering Russia, but Catherine dreamed of continuing his work someday.

After a few weeks of revelry, Czarina Elizabeth usually went to a monastery for a few weeks of prayer. Soon after the betrothal ceremony, she set out for the cathedral at Kiev with a retinue of two hundred servants. Catherine and Johanna were required to go with her, taking their place in the half-mile long entourage of courtiers, servants, and carriages.

In this engraving, hardworking serfs toil to build a log house.

As they traveled, Catherine began to see Russia in a new light. They passed fields where thousands of men and women labored under the sharp eye of an overseer with a whip. Under Peter the Great, any man who rose to a rank of commissioned officer in the military service automatically became a noble. These new nobles were allowed to buy estates, and with those estates came serfs—as few as a dozen for a poor man, as many as ten thousand for a rich one. Serfs were as much a possession as were furniture and clothing. According to some estimates, serfs comprised over ninety percent of the population in Russia at one point. Most of the country's wealth came from their labor. The serfs were no more than slaves, illiterate people condemned to toil for masters whom they might never see their entire, usually short, life. They barely eked out a subsistence living while their masters lived in luxury.

Catherine hardly had time to ponder what she had seen before they reached Kiev. Kiev was a city of monasteries, churches, priests, and catacombs. There, in a cathedral shining with gilt and diamonds, Catherine saw the most sacred relic of the Orthodox Church, a painting of Mary said to have been made by St. Luke. Elizabeth joined other pilgrims in a procession, all of them walking barefoot and carrying heavy crosses. Moving slowly down the crowded streets, she was fascinated by the contrast of the gold robes and jeweled icons of the priests and the ragged beggars who hobbled along with palms outstretched for alms. She noted the city's cosmopolitan mix of monks and Jewish merchants, soldiers and friars, Polish noblemen and Georgian princes.

After returning to Moscow, Catherine was startled to feel, for the first time, the czarina's wrath. Elizabeth had learned that the grand duchess was spending inordinate sums of money. Elizabeth chastised her for being so foolish. Catherine had not given a thought to how much she was spending; she simply spent the money as she needed or wanted to. She had ordered a new wardrobe for herself—borrowed clothes might have suited a poor German princess, but certainly not a Russian grand duchess. She had spent freely on gifts for her mother, Peter, and her servants, in hopes of winning their favor. But when she reviewed her receipts, she realized Elizabeth was right. Catherine had no choice but to swallow her pride and promise to be more careful. She breathed a sign of relief when Elizabeth's anger passed.

No sooner had that danger been averted than Peter contracted smallpox, which was a disease that quite often ended in death. If Peter died, Catherine might be sent back to Germany with her mother, or, as was the custom of the day, put in a convent for the rest of her life. Elizabeth, despite her doctor's warnings about contagions, remained at Peter's side for nearly two months. From St. Petersburg, Catherine sent her fiancé long and loving letters. She was not fluent enough in Russian to write in that language, so she merely copied over the words written by her teacher. Peter might have preferred a few lines in his native German tongue but Catherine knew Elizabeth would be more pleased by letters written in Russian.

While Peter was ill, Catherine idled away her time in the court. She was aware of the gossip about her future if Peter died. One visitor during that time was a Swedish diplomat who had known Catherine when she was a child. Meeting her now, he was disappointed to see she was neglecting her intellect. He scolded her, "You think of nothing but clothes. Return to the natural inclination of your mind. Your genius was born for great deeds." Catherine realized he was right and began reading again with renewed vigor. She studied a wide range of books including history, novels, biographies, and philosophy.

She was relieved to hear that Peter had recovered. Her friends at the court who were familiar with smallpox tried to prepare Catherine for what to expect when her fiancé returned to St. Petersburg. Peter's valet even arranged for their first meeting to take place in a dimly lighted room. He dressed Peter in an elaborate wig and highly decorated clothes. Still, after Catherine entered the room, her hesitation to reach forward to embrace her fiancé was noticed by everyone. Then she fled in tears. Peter's disfigurement was worse than she had thought possible. Never handsome, he now had a swollen nose, watery eyes, red and bloated skin, and deep pockmarks. Later she wrote, "he had become quite horrid to look at." Perhaps the most horrible part was something Catherine could not see. Smallpox had attacked his brain, making him prone to fevers and leaving him even more emotionally unstable than before.

Her situation seemed to be worsening, but Catherine faced her future with determination. She never thought of going back on her promise to marry Peter. She was marrying Russia, not this obnoxious teenager. Years later, she described her method: "I evinced great respect for my mother, implicit obedience to the Czarina, marked consideration for the Grand Duke, and most assiduously sought the affection of the people."

She suffered another setback when Peter turned against her. He might have been bitter about the way she reacted to his deformity, or because Catherine was clearly Elizabeth's favorite. Whatever the reason, he decided that she was the source of his unhappiness; their old confidences were forgotten. Peter refused to see Catherine unless forced to by Elizabeth, who decided to set a date for the wedding before the groom stopped speaking to the bride altogether. It was time; Catherine had been in Russia a year and a half.

Elizabeth wanted to impress the visiting European dignitaries with the wealth and elegance of the Russian court. She sent out teams to study the latest in European dress and

The exchange wharf in St. Petersburg.

social protocol. She paid enormous salaries to French car-
penters, decorators, and cooks who came to St. Petersburg
to prepare for the wedding. When spring arrived and the
Russian rivers and harbors were navigable, shiploads of
goods poured into the city. Catherine and Peter's wedding
was to be a celebration for all the people of Russia. Elizabeth
made sure there would be food and drink outside the
cathedral for anyone to enjoy. As the day approached,
Catherine became nervous. She had no idea what to expect
from this next step in her life.

On August 21, 1745, the sixteen-year-old bride donned
a jeweled robe of silver. Its wide skirt was so heavy she could
barely move. As she struggled to walk regally in it a heavy
crown was placed on her head. Peter also wore silver;
diamonds sparkled from his sword hilt to the buckles of his
shoes. The parade accompanying them to the church included 120 coaches and dozens of scurrying aides. The
retinue took three hours to move the three blocks to the
church. Catherine held her head high and smiled and nodded
regally. After a wedding service of several hours and another
procession through cheering crowds in the streets, the

newlyweds sat down to a banquet of fifty courses in the Winter Palace, a huge baroque building on the banks of the Neva River.

When the wedding was over, there was no reason for Johanna to stay in Russia. Catherine was not sorry to see her go, although her mother represented her last link to her old life. Elizabeth gave Johanna a parting gift of 60,000 rubles, less than half what Johanna owed her many creditors. Catherine promised to pay off the rest of her debts, though her personal allowance was only 30,000 rubles a year.

Due to an uncorrected physical condition, probably phimosis (in which the foreskin is contracted around the tip of the penis), Peter was incapable of consummating his marriage. All it would have taken to fix the problem was a minor surgery. But he refused to be examined by a doctor and, consequently, did not know he could be helped. Instead, he covered his embarrassment by bragging publicly about his affairs with other women. Catherine did not know that her husband was still a virgin—she believed he found her repellant and refused to approach her bed. Peter fed her fears by ridiculing her publicly.

A few days after her marriage, Catherine came to a conclusion about the rest of her life with Peter. She wrote: "I would have been ready to like my new husband had he been capable of affection or willing to show any…[but I said to myself] if you love this man, you will be the most miserable creature on this earth…think of yourself, Madame." Peter became even more cruel and unkind toward her, so she did what she could to survive. She hardened her heart toward her husband and focused on preparing for her new role in life.

Catherine was amazed by how quickly her life changed once she was married to Peter. Instead of being feted with parties and balls, she became the object of derision and gossip. Most of the court heard Peter's boasts about his affairs, and though some pitied the new duchess, others enjoyed seeing the intelligent foreigner reduced to tears. Elizabeth, instead of being the loving protector Catherine had grown to depend upon, turned against her. She became paranoid that Catherine and Peter were plotting to remove her from power. She punished Catherine by having her favorite servants sent away and appointing a minder for her—a servant loyal to Elizabeth—who kept Catherine under close surveillance and reported back everything she said or did.

After the couple had been married a year, Elizabeth let it be known that she was upset Catherine had not yet produced an heir. She blamed the grand duchess for not making herself attractive enough to entice her husband. She made Catherine sign a pledge that she would, "by her sensible behavior, her wit and virtue, inspire a sincere love in his Imperial Highness [the Grand Duke] and win his heart and that by so doing may bring forth the heir so much desired for the Empire." Catherine did not dare to tell Elizabeth that she was still a virgin. She began suffering agonizing migraines that she believed were caused by her loneliness and frustration. Still, she did not waver from her course. She continued her study of Russian and regularly attended

Orthodox Church services. She kept her eye on government affairs, both national and international, and comported herself in such a way that even Elizabeth's sharp eyes could not find further fault.

In 1747, Catherine received the news that her father had died. She had not seen him since she left home at the age of fourteen, and his death affected her deeply. She suddenly realized how far away from home and family she was—and how alone. After a week of private mourning, Catherine was told that she had to make her regular appearances in court. She was not allowed to mourn any longer because her father had not been a reigning sovereign. As a personal favor, Elizabeth allowed Catherine to wear mourning clothes for six weeks, but her grief had to be kept to herself. Catherine lifted her head and obeyed.

3

An Apprentice to the Throne

Catherine began to learn about the real Russia. While everyone in Elizabeth's court wore the most fashionable clothes and covered themselves in jewels, they did not have the same refinement and manners of other European courts. When Peter the Great had eliminated the hereditary requirement for nobility he made social classes more permeable. Catherine was surrounded by dukes who had once been peasants and princes who had mucked out stables. Few had any formal education, and there was not yet a viable Russian art or literature. Even the grand palaces were shoddily and hastily built—rats and mice roamed freely while residents shivered in the gusts of cold air sweeping through the cracks in walls and doors. Behind the ostentation and gilt of the court, there was very little real substance.

Catherine realized that her marriage was just as shabbily

constructed. She did not dare tell anyone that when she spent nights with Peter, whom she now considered little more than a retarded adolescent, they played war games with the toys he loved so much. He ordered that she sit with him on the bed while he arranged his wooden soldiers into regiments and moved them through imaginary battles. He demanded she pretend to shout orders to them as he did. Catherine did as she was told, noting "it was not for me to correct him; I let him do and say what he pleased." When her minder knocked, suspicious about the noise, Catherine would help her husband hide his toys under the bed.

Catherine wondered if she was the only one at court who knew Peter tortured the spaniel dogs he claimed to be raising for hunting. No one else seemed to be troubled by how much alcohol he drank. Catherine remained loyal to Peter in public. She even kept her silence when she walked into their bedroom to find him in the process of hanging a rat for the "crime" of nibbling at one of his toys.

Bored and discouraged, eighteen-year-old Catherine changed her clothes eight or ten times a day and spent hours perfecting her hair and makeup. It pleased her to find she was becoming more attractive, and she wrote proudly, "I was improving in looks from day to day." Her growing beauty angered Elizabeth, who began to complain that Catherine was vain, conceited, and considered herself superior to the czarina. In the cruelest criticism of all, Elizabeth again accused her of being unable to produce a child.

It was during these years that Catherine built her strong character, learned to control her temper, and became disci-

The Grand Duchess Catherine is pictured here on horseback. *(The State Russian Museum.)*

plined and controlled. She listened to Elizabeth's criticism humbly and played the role of the obedient servant. She hid her frustration at the monotony of her life—the endless balls, frequent pilgrimages, and royal visits to Baltic ports and dockyards. She traveled without complaint, sleeping in tents or servant's quarters as instructed. She saw members of the court imprisoned or mysteriously disappear for their alleged roles in real or imaged plots, and resolved to steer clear of diplomatic intrigue. She continued her efforts to become as Russian as she could.

Though Peter showed no sexual interest in his young wife, Catherine had no shortage of admirers. Elizabeth herself had a number of lovers and an atmosphere of sexual liberty pervaded the court. Catherine flirted innocently with several handsome young men. Then, in the spring of 1752, she met Serge Saltykov, a military officer. Twenty-three-

year-old Catherine found this dashing young man irresistible. She loved to ride, and he accompanied her on long outings along the beaches of the Gulf of Finland. Though Saltykov was married to one of Catherine's ladies-in-waiting, he said his wife meant nothing to him. Catherine was the one he loved. In her

Catherine's first lover, Serge Saltykov.

memoirs, Catherine wrote, "I held firm during the spring and part of the summer. I saw him almost every day but did not alter my behavior toward him." But, by the end of the summer of 1752, they were lovers.

Saltykov had learned that after eight years of marriage both Peter and Catherine were virgins. By then it was common knowledge at court. He also knew about Peter's physical condition. Cannily, he got Peter drunk one night and convinced him to let a doctor perform the necessary operation. Afterward, the ever-vigilant Czarina Elizabeth sent a woman to deflower Peter to make sure the procedure had been a success. Then she pushed the grand duke and the grand duchess into bed together and the marriage was finally consummated. Now, if Catherine became pregnant, no one could say with certainty that Peter was not the father. She did become pregnant but before the official announcement was made she miscarried. In May 1753 she miscarried again.

Saltykov grew tired of his mistress and wanted out of the relationship. Catherine was devastated—she believed she truly loved him. The all-seeing Czarina Elizabeth discreetly informed Saltykov he would not be permitted to leave Catherine until she carried a baby to term. His instructions were clear. Elizabeth wanted an heir; and what Elizabeth wanted, she usually got. In February 1754, Catherine, pregnant again, was moved to the Summer Palace at St. Petersburg to await the birth of her child. Fear of another miscarriage was almost overwhelming, as was her separation from her lover. She confessed in her diary: "I could not get it out of my mind that everything was moving toward a separation between Serge Saltykov and myself."

On September 20, 1754, Catherine gave birth to a boy. A midwife washed him and wrapped him in swaddling clothes. A priest anointed him with holy water. Then Elizabeth snatched him away. Catherine was left alone with her attendants. Peter stopped in for just a moment and then left to receive the congratulations of his court. Catherine was ignored: she had fulfilled her duty and given her adopted country an heir.

For three days, the attendants who brought Catherine food told her of Elizabeth's obsession with the child, and of how he was pampered by dozens of attendants. He had been named Paul. Catherine did not dare ask too many questions about him because that might imply she mistrusted Elizabeth's care of the infant.

Her son's birth was the cause for rejoicing all across Russia. Czarina Elizabeth had made it clear as soon as Catherine announced her pregnancy that she believed the child to be a legitimate heir to the Russian throne—Elizabeth might have even preferred an infusion of fresh blood from the vigorous and handsome Saltykov—and the infant was given the title grand duke. As a putative descendant of the Romanov dynasty, the Russian imperial fam-

Paul was immediately removed from Catherine's care and raised by his grandmother for most of his childhood. *(The Hermitage Museum.)*

ily that had ruled the country throughout much of the seventeenth century, and then again in the eighteenth century starting with Peter the Great, Elizabeth decreed that Paul would someday become emperor. The celebrations lasted for months.

Elizabeth presented the new mother with one hundred thousand rubles and what Catherine described as "a very meager necklace made up of small stones...such as I would have been ashamed to give a maid." Catherine was glad to have the money, though, for she had many debts. She understood her role in the royal family: she had produced an heir, and had been paid. Saltykov, his duty complete, was sent away to Sweden.

Catherine felt more alone and unwanted than she ever had, but was determined not to buckle under the circumstances. She knew the whole court whispered that her husband loathed her, her baby had been taken away, and her lover was gone. Catherine knew that if she were going to survive, it would be on the strength of her wits: "I resolved to make it plain to those who had caused me so many various sorrows that it lay in my power to see that I was not offended with impunity." For her next appearance in court, the first since Paul was born, she dressed in her finest clothes: "I walked with my head high, more like the leader of a great faction than like one humiliated and crushed." Gone was the innocent girl who had come to Russia believing a glorious future awaited her. In her place was a mature woman, perceptive and intelligent, who still believed in a glorious future—but one she would have to make for herself.

Catherine again turned to books. Ignored by her husband, the czarina, and most of the court, she resumed her study of European and Russian history and politics. She kept her eyes and ears open both to matters of routine administration and to matters of international importance, such as ongoing conflicts with Denmark and Prussia. She resigned herself to seeing her son only on state occasions.

There were some people at court who took pleasure in Catherine's humiliation, but a growing number felt sympathy for her. Although her affair with Saltykov had been an open secret, compared to the licentious Elizabeth, Catherine was a model of decorum and modesty. She continued to comport herself as a Russian, which made a pleasant contrast to Peter's growing obsession with Prussia.

Many Russians hated everything Prussian. This was partly due to fear of Prussian military might and the expansionary policies of Frederick the Great. Prussia, Austria, and Russia were all anxious to take advantage of the collapse of the Polish government. There were ongoing tensions along Prussia's eastern border. But much of the resentment toward Prussia grew out of the perceived influence Frederick and other Prussian rulers had on the Russian ruling family. Had he not even arranged the marriage of the future czar and czarina of Russia, who were both German-born?

Russia held a peculiar position in European affairs. Both Asian and European, the vast country had long been considered to be a backward, sleeping giant. Attempts to modernize were resisted. There was still deep resentment about Peter the Great's efforts to turn Russia toward Europe and to modernize his country. These so-called Old Believers resented being told their ways were wrong. The Russian Orthodox Church realized that Peter was a threat to its domination and control of the hearts and minds of the Russian people and became his most formidable foe.

Peter the Great had turned to Western Europe, especially Prussia, as a model of the type of reforms he wanted to impose on Russia. He admired the higher levels of literacy and innovation in Prussia, as well as its military prowess. Many years of his reign were spent in war with Sweden and Poland and he was often forced to turn to Prussia for support. This led to resentment toward the Prussian influence in the royal family and the intermarriage that had resulted in a German-born czar and czarina.

Not only the Old Believers, however, were insulted by the sight of Peter, the heir to the Russian throne, strutting about the palace in full Prussian military dress. He had made no effort to integrate into Russian life and missed few opportunities to exclaim on Prussian superiority in all things. The grumbling about Peter increased when he brought a regiment of soldiers from his home state of Holstein—which he technically ruled—to Russia. Holstein was very much in the Prussian sphere of influence and Peter was thrilled to be in the company of German-speaking men and spent all his time marching them up and down the palace grounds. He had a grand time taking marches around the countryside, bunking in with his troops and living with them in tents. Catherine quietly let it be known that she disapproved of her husband's Prussian obsession.

A portrait of Count Stanislas Augustus Poniatowski by Lampi. *(The Hermitage Museum.)*

News of Peter's insulting behavior spread. When British ambassador Sir Charles Hanbury-Williams visited Russia to renew the Anglo-Russian alliance, he ignored Peter and focused on Catherine. He knew Saltykov, Catherine's former lover, had been sent abroad and hoped to win her to the side of England by introducing her to a charming new lover. Catherine, who had told her diary "my heart cannot be content, even for an hour, without love," was quickly infatuated with Williams' choice. The Polish Count Stanislas Augustus Poniatowski was intelligent, cultivated, well read, and handsome. During the winter of 1755-56, Catherine and Poniatowski spent hours in secret meetings, moonlit drives along the frozen Neva River, and private assignations in her apartments.

The usually practical Catherine was swept away by her passion for her new lover. The couple lived in a fantasy world until the night of July 6, 1756. That evening,

Poniatowski set out to visit Catherine wearing, as usual, a blond wig and a mask. Peter caught him sneaking into the palace and brought the intruder to Catherine, demanding to know what was going on. Catherine trembled with fear, and then, much to her surprise, Peter began to laugh. He was joking, he told the startled lovers. He knew they were having an affair, and he did not care. He just thought it would be funny to pretend to be angry. To their further surprise, Peter insisted the stunned couple accompany him to his rooms to join him and his mistress for dinner. Catherine had long known about Peter's mistress, but had never anticipated eating a late-night, intimate dinner with her.

Since his operation, Peter had pursued several different women. After the dinner he again seemed to treat Catherine as an obliging older sister—this time, one that could give him advice about courtship. He began to come to her and demand help planning an evening tryst or decorating his rooms. Catherine handled him like a pesky younger brother. Once, when he filled his bedroom with guns and bayonets to impress a woman, she told him she thought his new mistress would take as much pleasure as he did in the room's décor.

Peter's mistresses were usually unpleasant women, no more intelligent than he was, and Catherine took no pleasure in their dinners together. But Peter liked Poniatowski and began to take him into his confidence. He told the startled count that he would have been much happier as an officer in the Prussian military than as "the Grand Duke of this cursed country."

The British Ambassador Sir Charles Hanbury-Williams.

Pleased that the affair with Poniatowski was working out so well, Hanbury-Williams took further steps to tie Catherine closer to England. She was always in debt because of her taste for luxury and her fascination with gambling so he gave her secret "loans" of thousands of rubles. She accepted the money, although she had to realize it left her open to a charge of treason.

In late 1756, Frederick II, Emperor of Prussia, invaded the German state of Saxony, beginning what became known as the Seven Years War. Elizabeth, who had grown deeply anti-Prussian, aligned Russia with France and Austria. England sided with Prussia and ambassador Hanbury-Williams returned to London. Catherine was sorry to see him go and took the risk of writing to him to promise she would do everything in her power to reunite England and Russia. She also provided him day-do-day accounts of Elizabeth's deteriorating health and wrote to him, "It is my dream to see her die....Make me Czarina, and I will give you comfort."

Elizabeth's years of overeating and drinking were catching up with her, but she also remained a fighter. She would become ill and appear to be on death's door, then seemingly bounce back. Each time her health recovered Catherine's plans and hopes were dashed, at least temporarily. Rumors began to swirl that Elizabeth would make Catherine's son Paul her heir, eliminating Peter from the line of succession. Catherine worried that if this happened she would be sent to a convent—or worse. As Elizabeth's health continued its frustrating, erratic decline, the succession question loomed larger. Catherine wrote in her journal, "I have already laid my plans and shall either perish or reign."

The next year, 1757, Elizabeth sent troops to fight the Prussians. The Russian army was large but poorly trained and miserably equipped. Despite this, Prussia was on the verge of a disastrous defeat when, unaccountably, the Russian troops retreated. Elizabeth flew into a rage. Most ominously, she was convinced Peter had ordered the retreat and that he and Catherine were planning to overthrow her.

Elizabeth's suspicions were not unfounded. Her own chancellor, Aleksi Bestuzhev, had approached Catherine about the subject of succession. He drew up a paper that said that upon Elizabeth's death, Peter would assume the throne and Catherine would share power equally with him—and that Bestuzhev would command the army and navy. Catherine was flattered that Bestuzhev recognized her as a potential leader, but knew it was dangerous to scheme with members of the court while Elizabeth was still alive. Besides, she had no intention of sharing power with Peter. She told her diary, "I regarded his plan more or less as the ramblings of a dotard."

In December 1757, Catherine gave birth to a daughter, whom Elizabeth named Anna after Peter's mother. She was acknowledged as a Romanov, though her father was probably Poniatowski. As she had done with Paul, Elizabeth took the infant away from Catherine soon after her birth. Catherine did not complain. She said only that she wanted to be made comfortable during her convalescence and to have the freedom and privacy to entertain as she wanted. She took comfort in the constant attention and adulation she received from Poniatowski.

Catherine's spirits were at their lowest ebb. She suffered almost constant harassment from the grand duke and Elizabeth presented only stony silence. She was not allowed to see her children, all her mail was intercepted and reviewed by the czarina's secret police, and she could hardly leave her room without being watched. One night, as she prepared to go to the theater—one of the few entertainments left to her—Peter burst into her room and ordered her not to go out. He was involved with one of her ladies-in-waiting and if Catherine went to the theater, her attendants would have to go with her. Peter wanted his mistress to stay in with him, so he told Catherine she would have to stay in too. It was the last straw for the frustrated duchess and she refused. Then, after her temper cooled, she began to fear that Peter would report their argument to Elizabeth.

Catherine decided to strike first. Still fuming, Catherine sat down at her writing table and wrote Elizabeth a letter.

She begged to be sent away from Russia forever. Life, she said, was unbearable for her. She could not possibly make Peter happy, and had been a disappointment to them all. What Catherine wanted, of course, was nothing more than to stay in Russia. She was asking Elizabeth to either send her away, which was not likely, or place her in a more secure position. In effect, calling her bluff. It was a terrible gamble. After giving the letter to a page, she could only hope her ploy would work.

Catherine heard nothing from the czarina for several weeks. She steeled herself to wait patiently. When she could not bear the stress of waiting, she took to bed and called for a priest—but not just any priest, Elizabeth's personal confessor. When he arrived, they were left alone for private conversation. The priest was sympathetic to Catherine's plight and agreed to use his influence with the czarina. The next day she was granted an audience.

Catherine knew the meeting would determine her fate. Upon entering the room, she saw Peter standing behind Elizabeth's chair smiling smugly. Piled on Elizabeth's desk were the secret letters Catherine had exchanged with Bestuzhev about succession. Certain her future held only prison or worse, Catherine put everything she had into one final performance. She fell to her knees and begged Elizabeth to let her go back to her family in Germany. She said she would leave her children in Elizabeth's care. When Elizabeth pointed to the letters and accused her of scheming to gain the throne, Catherine used every ounce of wit she had to redirect the czarina's ire. Perhaps because of her age, her illness, or her desire to believe what Catherine said, Elizabeth began to relent.

Sensing that Catherine was getting the best of the conversation, Peter could not resist jumping in to offer criticisms of his wife. He accused her of being proud, haughty, and of taking lovers behind his back. Catherine countered that Peter was scheming to get rid of his lawful wife so he could accept the crown with his mistress after Elizabeth was dead. Peter's shrill voice and hypocritical accusations of adultery turned Elizabeth against him. She ended the meeting by telling Catherine that she wanted to meet with her alone and soon. Catherine detected reason and gentleness in her voice. The barriers between them seemed to have been broken; but only their next meeting would tell for sure.

As before, several weeks went by with no message from Elizabeth. Catherine again began to talk about leaving the country. By now she felt confident Elizabeth would not want to risk the public embarrassment of letting her go. Her ploy paid off and the czarina called her in for an interview. She was even allowed to meet with her children for a few minutes beforehand. That reunion was bittersweet—they hardly knew their real mother, and she had few maternal feelings for these strangers. Her interview with the czarina was more productive. The two women came to a kind of peace. Elizabeth offered to let Catherine see her children once a week and Catherine consented to having her lover Poniatowski sent away.

Catherine's big gamble had worked. She would not be expelled from Russia. But bad news followed quickly on the heels of good when, a few months later, little Anna became sick and died. Then word came that Catherine's mother had died. To avoid scandal, Catherine had to beg Elizabeth to pay off her mother's final debts. Thirty-year-old Catherine found just two glimmers of hope in her future. One was that Elizabeth was still very ill. She suffered from heart problems brought on by obesity and too much alcohol.

The other advantage she had was that Peter was more unpopular than ever—especially with the army. As the European war entered its third year, Prussia had sustained so many losses that its army was reduced to a fraction of its strength. It was a terrible struggle. In one battle alone more than ten thousand men on each side were killed. Although she was very ill and in tremendous pain, Elizabeth vowed to continue the fight. It was an open secret that Peter was doing anything he could to help Frederick II, including passing on all the information he could gather from his spies in the Russian officer corps.

Catherine disassociated herself from her husband by openly disapproving of his behavior and friends. She sought out provincial governors and asked them to tutor her about Russia. She talked with older women who instructed her on Russian time-honored traditions and customs. She invited people to her drawing room that had knowledge of what was going on in Russian cities and towns and throughout the countryside. She told her doctor wistfully that she wished he could bleed her to her "last drop of German blood so that I may have only Russian blood in my veins."

In the summer of 1759 Catherine was introduced to the

Orlov brothers, five tall, handsome, and adventurous men—
Gregory, Ivan, Alexis, Feodor, and Vladimir. Gregory, at
twenty-four, was the most attractive and charming. Like his
brothers, he was devoted to Russia and already a decorated
military hero. He and Catherine soon began an affair. The
Orlov brothers were immensely popular and the affair
helped to cement her support within the Russian army.

Catherine remem-
bered well that Eliza-
beth had claimed the
throne at the head of
her troops.

Though Gregory
gave Catherine much
pleasure, and was a
valuable ally, he, like
most of her lovers,
was chosen more for
his appearance than
his intellect. After
spending passionate
and exciting time
with him, Catherine

Gregory Orlov. *(The State Russian Museum.)*

would retire to her
room to compose long thoughtful letters to the exiled
Stanislas Poniatowski.

Catherine found more unlikely allies at court. Count
Nikita Panin, young Paul's tutor, was smart and savvy. He
approached her to discuss the chaos that might follow

Elizabeth's death. Panin knew, as did Catherine, that Peter planned to divorce her, declare Paul illegitimate, and assume the throne with his mistress. Peter did not seem to understand or care that people at court were talking openly about his lack of intellect, his drunkenness, his

Nikita Panin, young Paul's tutor and an ally of Catherine's.

obsession with toy soldiers, and, most damaging, his support of Prussia and open scorn for the Russian Orthodox Church. Panin believed it would be both necessary and easy to get rid of Peter and to set up a regency for Paul that could be presided over by Catherine. While Catherine pretended to consider his plan, she had no intention of ceding power to her son when he reached maturity.

As the court began to splinter between those who backed Peter and those who backed Catherine, she found another supporter. Princess Dashkova was the seventeen-year-old sister of Peter's current mistress. As pretty and charming as she was impulsive and determined, Dashkova was ostracized from her family after she offered her support to Catherine. But the princess was enamoured of the grand

A cameo and seal of the Princess Dashkova. *(The Hermitage Museum.)*

duchess and fervently believed she should be the next ruler of Russia.

The Russian court was in turmoil. Every day new reports of casualties arrived from the front. Elizabeth was extremely ill and her doctors agreed she was probably dying this time. Peter made no secret of his intention to take the throne without his wife, if possible. Catherine had recently discovered she was carrying Orlov's child. She had to keep her pregnancy hidden. No one would think it was Peter's child. He could accuse her of infidelity and possibly even have her arrested. The winter of 1761 was tense, as everyone waited to see what their futures would hold.

By December, it was clear the Czarina Elizabeth was at death's door. On December 23, she suffered another series

The Grand Duchess Catherine secretly pregnant and in mourning for Czarina Elizabeth. *(The Tretyakov Gallery.)*

of strokes and asked for the last sacraments. The czarina died on Christmas Day, 1761.

The day after Elizabeth's death, Czar Peter III assumed the throne of Russia. No mention was made of his wife or son. Although his subjects were unhappy that he was the new ruler, and rumors of possible coups swirled, he ascended the throne without incident. Peter proudly seated his mistress at his side and accepted the homage of his people.

In her seventeen years in Russia, Catherine had learned patience as well as political skills. Though her supporters begged her to authorize a coup immediately, she refused. Only she knew why—the baby in her womb had to be hidden at all costs. She put on mourning clothes large enough to hide her pregnancy and kept vigil at Elizabeth's coffin.

Czarina Catherine

The public mourning for Czarina Elizabeth lasted ten days. Despite the fact she was six months pregnant, Catherine knelt at the foot of Elizabeth's coffin the entire time as thousands of people paraded by to pay their last respects. All of Elizabeth's subjects were invited to bid her farewell; Catherine's reputation spread quickly. This display of modesty and humility earned the admiration of all those who saw her. A French ambassador said of her, "no one is more assiduous in the performance of the duties due to the late Czarina.... the clergy and the people believe her to be deeply affected and are grateful to her on that account." The few times Peter appeared he ridiculed the priests, flirted with the ladies, and played the clown. He laughed during the funeral and pretended to chase after the coffin, ridiculing even the idea of grieving for the dead czarina. His hysterical antics bewildered and disgusted the court and the people.

In the first days of his reign, Peter made a quick peace with Prussia, violating the sentiments of patriotic Russians. He treated his mistress as though she were the reigning czarina. He declared publicly that Paul

Peter III after becoming czar.

was not his son and that he planned to marry his mistress. In an attempt to gain the support of the nobles, he exempted them from military and civilian responsibilities. He further antagonized the military by appointing his uncle, Prince George of Holstein, as commander in chief, and by requiring soldiers to dress in Prussian uniforms. He alienated the leaders of the Orthodox Church by turning Elizabeth's private chapel into a Lutheran church. He ordered the priests to adopt western clothes, confiscated church lands and other property, and proclaimed that all clergy were now employees of the state. Outraged, they denounced him as a heretic.

The new czar announced that he was taking command of the army and was planning an attack against Denmark, which had been in a long dispute with Russia over North Sea ports. He transformed the city into a garrison and spent hours drilling his troops, much the same way he drilled his toy soldiers. He commanded the artillery to fire day and night because the cannon booms thrilled him. He was usually drunk and seemed utterly heedless of the resentment his behavior was brewing.

Peter exiled Catherine to a remote wing of the palace, which secretly pleased her. As her pregnancy neared full term, she made arrangements to protect herself and her baby from Peter and the court. With the help of a few loyal servants, Catherine concocted a story that she had sprained her ankle and needed to stay in bed to heal. The night her labor pains began, she ordered a servant to set fire to a wooden building in town. She knew that Peter loved to watch fires and, as she hoped, he ran out to witness the conflagration. While he was gone, Catherine delivered another son whom she called Alexis. The newborn was wrapped in blankets and slipped out of the palace. He was taken to the home of a distant relative who had agreed to raise the boy as her own. Catherine had no time to be a mother.

Though she managed to hide her son from her husband, Catherine knew it was only a matter of time before he found an excuse to have her sent to prison or executed. In June of 1762, he invited four hundred guests to a banquet in honor of the peace treaty he had signed with Prussia. When Peter proposed a toast to the imperial family, Catherine remained seated. Furious, he demanded to know why she did not stand. She answered calmly that it was improper for her to stand when a toast was being drunk in her honor. Peter lost control and shouted down the length of the table that she was an idiot. The guests were stunned. Four days later, Peter gave the order to have her arrested. Though his advisors managed to talk him out of it, his intentions were now clear for everyone to see. If she was going to survive, Catherine had to act soon.

In 1722, Peter the Great had decreed that succession would no longer automatically be granted to the oldest member of the ruling family. Each ruler could name his own successor. Elizabeth, however, had not named a successor. Catherine believed she had as much right as Peter—and more ability—to claim the throne. Peter had not yet bothered to have himself officially crowned as czar, a step of enormous symbolic importance to the people of Russia.

Catherine began to plot her move. Gregory Orlov and his four brothers held important positions in the armed forces. They worked to win support for Catherine among the officers. They hoped to have over ten thousand men ready to fight on her behalf if necessary. Paul's tutor Panin and the young Princess Dashkova were loyal to Catherine and worked to bring other members of the court to her side. Most of the nobles and powerful church officials looked more favorably on Catherine than on Peter, but it remained to be seen how many of them would actually risk supporting her when the time came.

The view today of the house near the palace of Peterhof, later called the Catherine Block.

Catherine spent five days in St. Petersburg coordinating her plans. She tried to get support from foreign rulers and to raise money to finance her coup. She turned first to France for support. King Louis XV was reluctant to back her openly, worried about what would happen if she failed. The English, however, were happy to provide her with cash.

Catherine retreated to a secluded house near St. Petersburg where messengers could arrive without having to pass by palace sentries. One false move or remark could lead to the arrest of her fellow conspirators for treason. She wondered who would come first—Peter's henchmen to arrest her or a messenger from the Orlovs telling her it was time to make her move.

Alexis Orlov came first. He arrived in the middle of the

night and instructed Catherine's maid to awaken her. Alexis told her one of her supporters had been arrested. The unfortunate man had had too much to drink and made disrespectful remarks about Peter. It was only a matter of time before torturers forced him to reveal the plot. In a matter of minutes, Catherine was in a carriage to St. Petersburg. As they neared the city, Gregory Orlov appeared and rode along beside them for a few moments. He promised Catherine success, then dashed ahead to announce the coming of the new czarina. A little after seven o'clock in the morning, the carriage stopped and Catherine stepped out. She wore a simple black mourning dress and left her hair unadorned to show her respect for the late czarina.

Little Sophia from Germany, a Lutheran daughter of unimportant parents, was about to claim the throne of Russia. Catherine's first stop was a barracks. As soon as she emerged from the coach, the waiting soldiers began to cheer. The regiment's commander stepped forward to offer her his support and to declare her the new czarina of Russia. This simple ceremony was repeated at barracks all along the road to St. Petersburg.

As Catherine approached the Cathedral of Our Lady of Kazan, the cheering grew louder. Horse guards and elite regiments offered their allegiance. The soldiers saluted, drums beat out a welcome. Cheers of "Hurrah for our Little Mother Catherine!" rose in the air. People flooded the streets, laughing and crying, delirious at the sight of their new czarina whom they believed would bring them peace and prosperity.

At nine o'clock in the morning, Catherine knelt before the high altar to be blessed by the archbishop who proclaimed her to be Catherine II of all Russias. As she had ordered, prayers were said for eight-year-old Paul, now Czarevich Paul, whom she named as her successor.

After the ceremony, the new czarina appeared on the balcony of the Winter Palace holding Paul's hand, his blond curls shining in the sunlight. The crowd broke into frenzied cheering. With that appearance, Catherine acknowledged the existence of her son, claimed his legitimacy, and also established her status as ruler. Back at the palace, people surged up the grand marble staircase, eager to pay homage to Catherine. Princess Dashkova was boosted through the crowds and stood beside the new czarina as the manifesto announcing her reign was read aloud.

Catherine had written the manifesto. It was carefully written to appeal to the mass of Russian people as well as to the powerful nobility. It began by stating that the Orthodox Church had been "exposed to extreme danger by the course of recent events." She promised to return the Church to its position of supremacy in the country. The second point concerned, "the glory of Russia which…has been trampled underfoot by the conclusion of peace with our most mortal enemy [Prussia]." She promised to break Peter's alliance. When she finished reading the manifesto, troops paraded before her, shouting, "Long live our Little Mother Catherine! We are ready to die for her!" The first phase of the coup was a success.

Catherine expected Peter to march on the capital to fight

for his throne. Although she had taken precautions to keep her plans secret, there was always the chance that some other ambitious member of court or officer had learned of the coup and revealed it to Peter. The death of Elizabeth had unleashed ambition. Furthermore, she was heavily out-

Order of Saint Catherine medal granted to Princess Dashkova for her help in the coup.

numbered. She had only four regiments loyal to her; Peter had nominal control of a much larger force. If she were in his place she would mount a horse and enforce her claim to the throne.

When Peter found out about Catherine's coup later that afternoon he began to cry. Realizing that he was no match for his determined wife, Peter's advisors convinced him to board a ship and make for Kronstadt, a port city where much of the navy was anchored. But Catherine had already sent emissaries to the Russian Navy to ask the admirals to recognize her as czarina. When Peter's ship tried to enter the harbor at Kronstadt it was repulsed. The navy was loyal to Catherine; her emissaries had beaten Peter to the city. Peter's advisors told him to disembark anyway—the troops would not dare to shoot at him—but the ousted czar was weeping and cowering in the ship's hold. He refused to move. His ship had no choice but to return to Peter's summer residence. His advisors tried to convince him to gather his troops and fight, but by afternoon Peter was too drunk to respond. Disgusted, they left him.

Catherine borrowed a uniform from one of her soldiers. With her long hair floating down her back, splendid in the green uniform of a grenadier, the new czarina swung astride a magnificent white horse and rode out to review her troops. Holding an unsheathed sword aloft in her right hand, Princess Dashkova in uniform beside her, Catherine scrutinized the rows of soldiers. She expressed her satisfaction at their preparedness and told them to be ready to fight. They responded with a deafening cheer.

Catherine, always a staunch supporter of the Russian military, commissioned this dress to match the uniforms of the Prebazhensky Life Guards Regiment. *(The Hermitage Museum.)*

The next morning, Catherine received a message from Peter. He acknowledged his cruelty to his wife, promised to make amends, and offered to share his throne with her. Peter was not going to fight. Catherine was so

Catherine, in military dress, leading her army on a white horse, looking much as Elizabeth had in the stories told to Catherine on her first journey to Russia. *(Courtesy of Art Resource.)*

relieved she broke out in laugher. Peter's messenger quickly knelt before the new czarina and swore his loyalty to her.

Catherine responded to Peter's letter by insisting he sign a statement announcing his unconditional abdication immediately. She had to decide what to do with her husband. She did not want to confine him in a prison for fear he would become a symbol for her enemies to rally around. But if she had him killed he could become a martyr and symbol of her betrayal. She ordered that he temporarily be exiled to his country estate in Ropsha, outside of St. Petersburg, and kept under guard. He was stripped of his uniform and sword and separated from his mistress. She instructed her guards to be kind to him.

On June 30, 1762, Catherine rode into St. Petersburg, still dressed in her uniform, at the head of her troops. Crowds greeted her with cheers and banners. Members of the Holy Synod, gowned in their most splendid robes, blessed her as she entered the city gates. Church bells pealed and military bands blared. Catherine had succeeded in a nearly bloodless seizure of power. She was ready to accept the world's admiration. As one writer described her, "her figure is noble and agreeably impressive; her gait majestic; her person and deportment graceful in the highest degree. Her air is that of a sovereign."

The Russian treasury was dangerously low but Catherine ordered that her favorite advisors and military officers be showered with money and presents. Gregory Orlov received 50,000 rubles, soldiers at the garrisons that supported her were each granted half a year's salary, and the list went on and on. In accordance with Russian tradition, she also distributed serfs, or souls. There seemed to be no end to the number of souls Catherine could grant. Each of the Orlov brothers received eight hundred serfs; the foster parents of her youngest son received a thousand; eleven leaders especially prominent in the coup received six hundred serfs each.

While Catherine was still trying to decide what to do with Peter, she received a hastily written note from Alexis Orlov that made her fear her short-lived period as czarina might be over. While under heavy guard, Peter had been killed. Orlov was vague about how it happened. He begged for Catherine's forgiveness while admitting that he and the other members of Peter's guard should be put to death. Catherine brushed aside his protests, as he no doubt expected her to, and demanded an explanation. What she heard made her furious. Peter had been murdered, and it appeared that Alexis Orlov had planned it. "My reputation is ruined," she cried, "never will posterity forgive me for this involuntary crime!"

Though it troubled Catherine that Peter's blood was on her hands, she did what she thought needed to be done to cover up the crime. She wrote and published an edict stating that Peter, who had suffered from hemorrhoids, had died after a particularly severe attack. This public explanation was not very convincing, but it was nevertheless accepted. The rumors that Peter had been poisoned were a stroke of good luck. She ordered the autopsy doctors to look for signs of poisoning. If they found none, they were to rule the death accidental. There was no need to report on anything else

This guilded carriage belonged to Catherine and is thought to be the one that returned her to the palace after her coronation. Today it is kept in the Hermitage Museum in St. Petersburg. *(Courtesy of Art Resource.)*

they found in their examination, such as marks on the neck that would suggest strangulation. The doctors found no sign of poison and ruled the death accidental. A relieved Catherine again donned black mourning clothes to express her grief publicly.

It was important to hurry on with official business. As Catherine made preparations for her coronation, she needed the country to appear as stable as possible so her reign would be accepted abroad. From the moment she was declared czarina, overseas governments had been mostly pleased but necessarily cautious. Her husband had reigned for only a few months. Who knew how long she would survive?

In the summer of 1762, as thirty-three-year-old Catherine prepared for her coronation in Moscow, she was determined that her subjects would be treated to a spectacle. She chose Moscow as the site because it would please the more conservative and patriotic Old Believers. It was the capital of Russia before Peter the Great had moved it to St. Petersburg and had a long political and religious history. She provided her supporters with both money and the freedom to produce a memorable event. She sent designers a pound of gold and twenty pounds of silver to be used to make her crown and four thousand ermine skins for her cape and its long train. She arrived in Moscow on September 13th with a retinue of twenty-three attendants with sixty-three coaches and wagons. Paul rode beside her in a gilded coach looking a little frightened and bewildered. He had been ill along the way but seemed to have recovered by the time he reached Moscow. The crowds cheered for both mother and son and followed them to the Cathedral of the Assumption, a church rich in Byzantine history and tradition, a magnificent building of golden icons, massive columns, and frescoed walls.

On September 22, 1762, Catherine slipped out of her ermine cloak and put on an imperial purple robe. She placed the heavy crown on her head and sat regally—a scepter in one hand and a jeweled globe with a cross on top in the other. The crowds knelt silently as the archbishop gave her holy unction and proclaimed her the head of the Orthodox Church. Eighteen years before, the teenaged Sophie had been formally engaged in this same church. Now she was crowned Czarina Catherine II.

Catherine returned to the palace in a golden coach. Her courtiers tossed silver coins to the crowds. Long tables were set up with great displays of food prepared for the citizens who attended the ceremony. As the people enjoyed the food and praised their new czarina, Catherine presided over a

Catherine's coronation on September 22, 1762.

banquet for dignitaries in the Granovitaya Palace, a fine example of Italian Renaissance architecture. That night, crowds hovered around the grandly lit Kremlin until Catherine appeared on the historic Red Staircase at midnight to accept their cheers.

Though her coronation was an impressive event, Catherine's main concern was the future of Russia. She planned to make Russia the most powerful country in the world. She had decided on this goal long before Elizabeth died. She had written in her journal, "To join the Caspian to the Black Sea and both to the North Sea; to establish trade routes from China and the East Indies through Tartary, would be to raise this Empire [Russia] to a degree of power above that of the other empires of Asia and Europe. And what can resist the unlimited power of an absolute prince who governs a warlike people?"

5

Building an Empire

For the next several days Catherine attended meetings, receptions, balls, and dinners. She appeared at a parade that stretched over a mile, a giant public masquerade, and a transvestite ball where a British envoy said of Catherine in her officer's uniform, "A man's dress is what suits her best." The downside of the festivities was that Paul suffered a relapse and for the third time that month was bedridden with a fever so high it made him delirious.

The international community was not quite sure what to make of the woman who had taken the throne of Russia from her own husband. To be sure, Catherine was the fifth woman to rule Russia in recent years, but no one was sure her reign would last. She was determined to show them it would. She set out her plan for the future and explained how she wanted to continue to modernize. Catherine's reading of the Enlightenment philosophers had convinced her that slavery was an evil. But she realized it would be politically and economically disastrous to try to change the system of serfdom overnight. She resolved instead to try to make the lives of her subjects better gradually and hopefully, one day, end the barbaric practice.

When she learned about the terrible working and living conditions in the mines of the north, she decreed that no serf should be compelled to work there. When mine owners refused to go along with the decree, the serfs went on strike. Then, to keep the economy rolling, Catherine had to send in soldiers to suppress the strike. She made some attempts to investigate and alleviate the conditions of workers in the newly emerging industrial factories, but many local governors refused to work with her. She had inherited a government in which each department was riddled with bribery and corruption at every level. She could do little about the prevailing fraud because corrupt officials refused to investigate or indict other corrupt officials.

Catherine's first meeting with the Senate, an assembly of nobles, was an education in Russian politics. She learned that soldiers had not been paid in months. The budget was a mess; Russia was deeply in debt, and no one seemed to know what to do about it. Across the vast plains of the country were numerous peasant rebellions, and justice was merely an abstract word. Undaunted, she ordered a full report on every situation she knew about and assigned people to bring her information about the ones she did not know existed.

A commemorative ruble issued for Catherine's acension.

Catherine loved to work and wanted to control every aspect of the country both nationally and internationally. Her logical mind found paperwork appealing. She imposed order on her office staff and plunged into the business of cleaning up Russia. First, she needed to get some cash into the treasury. Russia had a unique monetary system: the currency was not backed by gold or silver or any other commodity, but only by the word of the reigning sovereign. Catherine could order more money printed without risking inflation—a step not possible in any other country. In addition, she declared that she would no longer accept the personal allowance granted to every Russian ruler. This saved almost a tenth of the country's total annual budget.

Once there was money in the state's coffers, Catherine set about bringing the Senate in line with her ideas. The Senate was a large body comprised entirely of men from the landed nobility. Most of them were significantly older than the new czarina and used to doing things in traditional ways. Catherine was quick to question their methods and introduce them to new and more efficient ways to run a government. Though some in the Senate resented all the changes, her insight, enthusiasm, and patriotism impressed most of them.

She never seemed to tire despite studying reports and diplomatic correspondence, meeting with department heads, and presiding over the Senate and ministerial councils for twelve to fourteen hours a day. Catherine believed that Russia needed a strong ruler because it was so vast that it was impossible to coordinate the decisions of the leaders of all the individual provinces. She credited Peter the Great for setting the example of a very active sovereign. To make sure that the Russian people saw her as a Russian, not a foreigner, she referred to Peter as "Our Grandfather Emperor Peter the Great." She

A drawing of Peter the Great. *(Amsterdam Museum.)*

let it be known that she idolized this ruler who had made the country into a European power, created a modern western capital, built a navy and reformed the army, emancipated women, introduced religious toleration, and developed commerce. Despite her declarations that serfdom was inhumane, she acknowledged that much that Peter the Great had accomplished could not have been done without slave labor.

Catherine established a few rules by which she hoped to govern. One was, "One should do good and avoid doing evil as much as one reasonably can

The writings and ideas of Enlightenment thinkers such as François Voltaire had a significant effect on Catherine.

out of love of humanity." Another was "to establish that courtiers should learn that the best way to flatter me is to tell me the truth." Her relationship with her subordinates was unusual for the honesty she encouraged from them. Rather than treating political positions as rewards for service, Catherine made it a point to nominate only the best and the brightest to her government—regardless of their backgrounds. Her overriding concern was not her own ego but the glory of Russia.

Early in her reign, Catherine commissioned French architect Vallon de la Mothe to build her a palace with a vast garden. The resulting Hermitage was the first real home she had since coming to Russia. Determined to bring European culture to her adopted country, she began collecting works of art and displaying them at the Hermitage. She began a rich and lively correspondence with the French Enlightenment leader Denis Diderot as well as his contemporary the writer and philosopher François Voltaire. Catherine impressed both these prominent figures with her liberal outlook. Voltaire soon came wholly under her spell and wrote volumes of poetry dedicated to her. Diderot encouraged artists, engineers, doctors, lawyers, and other professionals to travel to the rapidly growing Russian cities.

Catherine wanted to increase Russia's population. More people meant an economically stronger country, and Russia had more than enough space to accommodate an increase in population. She hoped to accomplish this goal in two ways: first, she wanted to improve the lives of her people so more of their children would live to see adulthood. In some remote villages, only one or two children out of ten would make it. Second, she hoped to lure German colonists to come to Russia to farm in the rich soil of the Volga, a

Under Catherine, the Smolny Institute became one of Russia's most important educational institutions. Much later, this elaborate structure would be the headquaters of the Bolsheviks during the tumultuous Russian Revolution of 1917.

region north of the Caspian Sea, and the Ukraine. She believed that the colonists would spread the German work ethic to the Russian serfs who had lost their ambition under the domination of their masters.

She also knew Russia needed a better-educated population. Catherine created naval and military schools, medical and agricultural schools, seminaries for priests, and an academy of drama. The most successful of her educational projects was the famous Smolny Institute for Girls in St. Petersburg. Catherine supervised the curriculum and made regular visits. The Institute focused on training each student's body and mind, a decided change from the narrow vocational system favored in other girls' schools. Catherine hoped to create a generation of educated and intelligent young women who would shape the next generation of Russian leaders.

After conducting a thorough and merciless inspection of Russia's internal issues, Catherine was able to turn her attention to foreign affairs. During the eighteenth century, many nations in Europe looked for ways to expand their borders. There were several powerful monarchs and the most destructive of the religious conflicts that had begun in the early sixteenth century had finally ended. Great Britain, France, Austria-Hungary, Prussia, Denmark and Russia all had expensive militaries that needed to be put to use. At the same time, previously powerful counties, such as Sweden and Poland, were only shadows of their former selves.

While waiting for her chance to rule, Catherine had studied the European situation. She had conversations with foreign diplomats and asked countless questions of Orlov and his friends in the army. They agreed that the lowest hanging fruit, the country that offered the best chance for expansion, was Poland.

Poland, on Russia's western border, had long suffered from internal dissension and a weak government. The Polish king Augustus III was elderly and ill. When he died, Catherine planned to take advantage of Poland's cumbersome system of government to put her own man on the throne. Though Poland was a monarchy, it was unusual because a council of nobility elected the monarch. Catherine began quietly buying allegiances within the Polish council and waited for the time to make her move.

Placing a handpicked king on the Polish throne would solve two of Catherine's problems at once. Ever since her husband's death, her old lover Stanislas Poniatowski had been besieging her with letters from abroad. Exiled since Elizabeth's time, Poniatowski begged Catherine to let him return and, he hoped, marry her. Catherine had no intention of marrying Poniatowski, or anyone else; she was perfectly content ruling alone. Though she tried to arrange a marriage for him behind his back as a way to get rid of him, he refused to go along with her plan. She finally decided to turn his obsession to her own advantage. She sent him a message that she needed him to wait patiently until she called on him to assume the throne of Poland. Poniatowski wrote back protesting that he had no desire to be king of Poland—he wanted only to be near her.

As Catherine was busy fending off Poniatowski's advances from abroad, Gregory Orlov was causing her trouble at home. Her handsome young lover was growing restless now that the new czarina spent so much time on her work. He was jealous of her state duties and took out his anger in affairs that he flaunted before Catherine. Though

An unfinished portrait of Gregory Potemkin by Lampi. *(The State Russian Museum.)*

she cared deeply for the soldier who had helped her gain the throne, she would not let her feelings for him interfere with her official business. Orlov would have to be patient. Catherine refused his petitions for marriage and put up stoically with his moodiness and flagrant infidelities. One of her most famous remarks, "I cannot live one hour without a man," helps to explain why she kept the difficult and often petulant Orlov in her court.

It was Gregory Orlov who introduced Catherine to the man who would become, in many ways, the closest she would ever have to a co-ruler. Gregory Potemkin was one of the soldiers who had ridden behind Catherine the day she overthrew Peter. He was a cheerful man who enjoyed pranks and lively conversation. But he was also shrewd, intelligent, and, unlike many members of the Russian nobility, energetic. Catherine was quick to recognize Potemkin's value. Orlov soon regretted introducing them, worried Catherine would drop him in favor of this new man. He lobbied Catherine to send Potemkin away from the court and, indulging her temperamental lover, she did for a while. But Potemkin came back; his advice and wisdom were more indispensable than Orlov's affection.

Not long after Catherine was crowned, at age thirty-three, rumors and complaints began to circulate. Some grumbled that Czarevich Paul should have been crowned in Catherine's place. When Paul became seriously ill, it was whispered that Catherine had poisoned him because she too believed that he was the legal heir to the throne. Paul recovered, but suspicion remained. Aware of this suspicion, Catherine was threatened by Paul's existence. She felt no strong maternal attachment to her son, nor did he have any love for his mother. For years, Elizabeth had allowed the two to see each other only sporadically, and mother and son were virtual strangers. But Paul was not the only threat—twenty-two-year-old Ivan VI still lingered in the wings.

A descendant of Peter the Great (he was Peter's great great nephew), Ivan's claim to the throne was stronger than that of the German Lutheran Catherine. Why was Ivan rotting away in a dark cell when he should be clothed in the purple and gold robes of Russian royalty? Other rumors circulated that Ivan was mad, and that those who wanted him on the throne planned to make him a puppet king.

Out of curiosity, Catherine went to see the young man at

the prison where Elizabeth had sent him. She reported that she found him "stammering and unintelligible in his speech and bereft of understanding." Having been kept in solitary confinement since the age of six, Ivan was uneducated and verging on insanity, but he never forgot that he was heir to the Russian throne. Catherine felt no pity at the sight of him or the conditions in which he was kept. After her visit she reaffirmed the standing orders that had been in place since Ivan was first sent to prison over fifteen years ago: if there was any attempt to abduct him from his cell, he should be killed instantly by his jailers.

Though Catherine wanted to avoid making enemies, she also wanted to make significant changes. One such change had to do with the role of the Orthodox Church. The church had long been an extremely powerful institution. Its leaders enjoyed many privileges and had grown accustomed to the perks of their positions. Catherine prepared to change this.

One of the central ideas of the Enlightenment was that religion had no place in government. Accordingly, she confiscated church property and placed it under the juris-diction of the government. This turned approximately 2,000,000 church officials into tax-paying citizens. The edict also took large expanses of land from the church. Archbishop Arsenius Matsievich, an influential church leader, openly called on parishioners to rebel against Catherine. He said she was a foreigner and not a true member of the church. In sermons, he called her a "murder-ess, assassin, usurper, and whore." Going against the advice of her aides, Catherine refused to bow to the archbishop.

Instead, she had Matsievich imprisoned and sentenced to a life of hard labor. Her gamble worked and the power of the Orthodox Church was dramatically weakened.

Catherine established the Commission on Commerce to study the flow of imports and exports. She wanted to simplify business procedures, remove obstacles to growth and innovation, and stimulate financial activity. The commission was astounded when Catherine presented it with a list of observations and possible projects and asked that they enlarge on her list and oversee its implementation.

In less than two years, Catherine accomplished a great deal. She encouraged immigration by granting new citizens temporary exemption from taxes and creating a special department to be responsible for their needs She supported agricultural projects in previously uncultivated areas of the country. This led to an increased food supply, higher tax revenues, and the creation of new markets for farm machinery. She brought schools and orphanages to the country and established Moscow's first public hospital offering free treatment to both men and women.

Catherine was known as a charming conversationalist and was as polite to her servants as she was to ambassadors from abroad. A British envoy said, "Her conversation is brilliant, perhaps too brilliant for she loves to shine in conversation. She does so to an uncommon degree, and 'tis almost impossible to follow her, her sallies are so quick, so full of fire, spirit, and vivacity."

One of the ways Catherine amused herself was by writing. She wrote anonymous pieces for a satirical journal titled *All Sorts and Sundries* and worked on plays, fiction, and poetry. Physically, long working hours and a big appetite meant that she grew stouter each year. One observer described her: "She has a fine mouth and teeth, and blue eyes, expressive of scrutiny...Her features are in general regular and pleasing." Though never conventionally beautiful, Catherine was an imposing and regal presence. Remembering the licentiousness that had permeated Elizabeth's court, she worked to keep her amorous adventures private. She led a more moderate lifestyle than Elizabeth had and kept a close watch on the people around her. She was quick to chastise anyone she caught telling a lie and barred all foul language and risqué jokes or stories from her court.

Smallpox had long terrorized the people of Russia. The disease had no cure and a high death rate. Catherine had seen what it had done to Peter before they were married. When she read about the invention of a vaccine that might prevent the illness, she was eager to bring it to her country. But the people of Russia would not likely volunteer to have a trace amount of the disease rubbed into a cut in their skin as a way of inoculating them—most of her subjects were highly superstitious and uneducated. In her typically direct fashion, Catherine decided she would have herself vaccinated.

Catherine's impending vaccination was a huge and momentous event. As the news of it spread, most people were certain she would die. Her advisors begged her to abandon the idea, but Catherine had done her research and firmly believed vaccination worked and would do much good for her country. She went ahead with the procedure. Gregory

Posters such as this one were used to encourage smallpox vaccination in Russia during Catherine's reign.

Orlov had himself inoculated too, bravely promising he would die with his mistress. In the days after her vaccination, Catherine insisted on conducting business as usual. She gave no sign that her confidence in the vaccine ever wavered and, once her doctors declared the experiment a success, she urged her subjects to follow her example.

In May 1764, Catherine received news that made her tremble. Ivan VI had been killed by his guards. An investigation uncovered papers showing that Ivan's supporters had been preparing to release him and to stage a coup in Moscow. The guards were following the orders they had been given to kill the prisoner should any attempt be made to abduct him from jail, but the event was a public relations nightmare. She had been on the throne for less than two years and was finally beginning to gain the respect of the international community and the support of her people. Now she was blamed for Ivan's death. Of course, many did not believe the coup story and were convinced that she had him murdered. Two claimants to the throne—Peter III and Ivan VI—had been killed in less than two years. Maybe Catherine was not the enlightened ruler she claimed to be. The man who had tried to abduct Ivan in order to restore him to the throne was captured and sentenced to death. Catherine did not commute his sentence, despite many pleas for mercy.

A few months later, word came from Poland that the king there had finally died. Catherine was privately anxious about the timing of his death, given her unpopularity because of the death of Ivan, but publicly she remained resolute. She had stationed 30,000 Russian troops on the border, ready to strike at a moment's notice if the Polish council did not do as she wished. When the Polish nobility unanimously voted to make Poniatowski their next king, he accepted the crown reluctantly. Catherine was thrilled. Before she had engineered Poniatowski's ascension, Catherine had consulted with Emperor Joseph II of Austria, who was her ally against Frederick the Great of Prussia, to ensure there would be no international opposition to Russian control in Poland. He had given her his blessing, though he had warned her to be discreet. "I will make a king as quietly as possible," she promised. Now, for all intents and purposes, Poland belonged to Russia. Poniatowski was ordered to sign treaties with terms favorable to Russia and did so without question. Catherine ignored the angry voices of dissent from the increasingly oppressed and patriotic Polish people. She cared only for the glory of Russia.

The part of Poland Catherine particularly coveted was

This contemporary map of Eastern Europe and Russia depicts current-day Belarus, the area that was once White Russia.

known as White Russia (today, Belarus), which contained 1.6 million people. Since 1386, it had been ruled by Catholic Poles, but the majority of people in the region had remained Russian Orthodox. In the last two hundred years, these so-called "White Russians" had become subservient to the Polish aristocracy. She insisted that this was an injustice that she was determined to alleviate.

Although Joseph II had promised that Austria would not contest Russia's advance into Poland, other European powers were not content to sit by and watch Catherine expand her territory. Turkey, Russia's Black Sea neighbor, was particularly incensed by Russian expansion. A long history of border and religious conflicts had made the two countries especially sensitive to each other's moves.

As events in Poland unfolded, Catherine worked on an ambitious plan to reform Russian laws. She was determined to review the existing legal system and amend it to make it more fair and accessible to officials and citizens alike. She set aside three hours each day for study. Over the course of two years, she compiled what she hoped would be the most important project of her life: a text of twenty-two chapters called *Instruction with a View to the Elaboration of a Code of Laws.*

The work was more of a philosophical treatise than a book of law. It suggested principles by which a Russian ruler should be guided when making decisions about the country's legal system. In creating it she drew heavily on her study of European philosophy and history, acknowledging a tremendous debt to her correspondent Voltaire and another French thinker, Charles Montesquieu. Twenty years earlier, Montesquieu had published *The Spirit of Laws,* a highly influential work about the proper role of government in a nation's affairs. The ideas he advocated, along with the writings of the Scottish philosopher John Locke and other Enlightenment political thinkers, were incorporated into the U. S. Constitution. Catherine wanted to implant these ideas into Russia. But it turned out to be more difficult to reform an existing country's legal and political system than it was to create a new one.

Catherine organized a Grand Commission, made up of 564 delegates from all the geographic areas of her empire to review her *Instruction.* Her idea was to present her plan to the representatives of the people in order to bring the government to those it governed. Although the commission did not even claim to speak for the serfs—the people who made up an overwhelming majority of the population—her subjects were surprised and delighted to think that their ruler cared about their opinions.

In the end, the commission took two years to pore over the document but did little else. The first several meetings were devoted to deciding upon the appropriate title to award Catherine for her dedicated service to the country. While she was pleased to become officially designated Catherine the Great, she eventually realized the commission would never approve her plan. The meetings were endless, stuffy, and unproductive—dominated by a few long-winded speakers and all but incomprehensible to most of those present. Few proposed votes passed.

Although it is true that many of the assembled could barely understand the complexites of the treatis she had written, the real problem was an overwhelming institutional resistance to change in Russia. The portion of the population who desperately wanted change was not even allowed to attend meetings. Why would a group of nobles and a few middle class merchants, the very people who profited so nicely from the current arrangement, be motivated to change it? Catherine was not willing to attempt to free the serfs. It would have been a highly risky move that could very easily have resulted in her removal. But without the support of the serfs she was unable to make fundamental change to the antiquated and highly inefficient Russian social and economic system.

Though Russia was not ready for the ideas in Catherine's *Instruction,* intellectuals in Europe were a far more appreciative audience. The *Instruction* was translated into several languages and its praises sung across the continent. Catherine was hailed as a model leader and enlightened ruler. The czarina misunderstood at home was celebrated abroad.

In December of 1768, Catherine regretfully announced that she had to disband the commission. Its members may have understood they were being dismissed because they were unable to accomplish the goals set for them, but the official reason was far more dramatic: Turkey had just declared war on Russia.

6

War

Russia's de facto control of Poland made much of Europe nervous. Some of the tension was sectarian. The vast majority of Poles were Catholic and Russia was Orthodox. Within Poland, a growing number resented Russian domination. The Turks, who shared a border with Poland, began to provide support to these rebellious Poles. By 1768, there was a vocal group of Poles who wanted to see Russia out of Poland and to see non-Catholic Poles kept in subservient roles. With Turkey's support, these nationalists made plans to take up arms against Russia.

Catherine was initially pleased at the growing power of these Polish dissidents. Because they threatened the civil rights of Polish citizens, she claimed to have no choice but to send in troops to keep the peace. She ordered 40,000 Russian soldiers in to subdue the rebels. They were instructed, she piously announced, to teach tolerance. When Russian troops briefly crossed the Turkey-Poland border and occupied a Turkish town, Turkey put the Russian ambassador to their country in jail and declared war.

Catherine was delighted to go to war with the Turkish Empire, which controlled several jewels Catherine hoped to snatch away. Most importantly, she wanted control of the Crimea, a peninsular region extending into the Black Sea. Russia had no warm water ports, which kept its naval and merchant ships landlocked during the long Russian winters. Access to the Crimea would change that. It would also extend Russian power farther into the Black Sea and the Caucasus Mountain region. The ultimate prize would be to recapture the city of Constantinople (Istanbul). Constantinople, the spiritual home of the Orthodox Church, had fallen to the Muslim Turks in 1453. The dream of restoring it to its Christian glory had been the dream of generations of Russian, and Greek, Orthodox believers.

The war started well for the Russians, who defeated the Turks in the first battle in the Dardenelles Straits that linked the Marmara and Aegean Seas. In July 1770, Russian ships destroyed the Turkish fleet in the Aegean Sea. Catherine gleefully described the battle: "They say that the earth and sea trembled with the huge number of exploding ships." The Russians bombarded Turkish strongholds on the Black Sea, a prelude to capturing Constantinople. But then the Russian momentum slowed and the war ground down to intermittent skirmishes with little gain for either side. Catherine sent long letters to her generals at the front flattering them and urging them to fight for glory. She grandly entertained officers on leave at the Winter Palace and showed up at military parades in full uniform.

Though the Russian advance had lost momentum, the success of Catherine's armies made an impression on the leaders of Europe. They decided not to openly oppose her on the battlefield, but the French, and even her ally Joseph II of Austria, were concerned about Russian expansion. If the Russians defeated the Turks, they feared there would be little that could stop Catherine from turning west and taking all of Europe.

Catherine too seemed convinced that Russia, with its enormous territory and population, was capable of anything. In one telling episode, she came across an enormous rock that captivated her. She decided to commission a statue of Peter the Great and make this tremendous rock its foundation. The only problem was that the rock was in

The people of St. Petersburg celebrate the unveiling of the equestrian statue of Peter the Great by the French sculptor Etienne Falconet in 1782. The name Peter comes from the Greek for "rock," and the impressive statue quickly became a symbol of the strength of the Russian empire.

Finland, and the czarina wanted the statue to stand in St. Petersburg. Undaunted, Catherine supervised an incredible undertaking. Over the course of a year, on a road

Catherine's statue of Peter the Great still stands in St. Petersburg today.

built just for this purpose, the three million-pound rock was put on a special contraption and pulled by one hundred horses all the way to Russia. This story of Catherine's determination became a legend.

In the face of such an indomitable ruler and people, it seemed inevitable that Turkey would soon be defeated. By 1770, most thought the war was all but over. Catherine began making plans to divide up Poland. Wishing to appease her European friends and secure their support, she arranged a secret conference with Frederick II of Prussia and Joseph II of Austria. In return for their cooperation with the invasion of Poland, she planned to reward each with a slice of the country. The ever-loyal Poniatowski assented to Catherine's plan and oversaw the fragmentation of what was supposed to be his kingdom. Catherine triumphantly received White Russia and its residents, while Austria and Prussia each obtained a healthy share of land and people.

The formal treaty of division announced that the partition of Poland was done "in order to reestablish order inside this country and to give it a political existence more in conformity with the interests of its neighbors." Polish nobles and peasants were humiliated and angry. Gradually, a rebellion grew within the country. Peasants used stones and sticks to attack the foreign invaders. Catholic priests urged their parishioners to march against the Lutheran and Orthodox soldiers occupying their country. England, France, Sweden, Spain, Italy, and the Vatican denounced the partition plan. But no one would go to war to support the Poles. Not only was Russia was a formidable foe, but Catherine had cleverly brought the powerful countries Austria and Prussia to her side by giving each a piece of the spoils.

Though the partition of Poland was a success, Catherine made a tactical error when Turkey initiated peace talks. Over the years she repeatedly made the same mistake of mixing business with pleasure. She often gave whichever man was first in her affections enormous power within her government—too blinded by her desire for him to realize the potential for danger. So when Turkey requested a meeting, Catherine sent the hot-headed and vain Gregory Orlov to negotiate for her.

Orlov quickly offended the Turks and behaved outrageously at the conference. When Catherine heard the reports of his actions, she was furious and, perhaps out of spite, took another lover. When word of her infidelity reached Orlov, he abandoned the talks and rushed three thousand miles to St. Petersburg to confront her. After a few heated exchanges, Catherine ordered him to leave her court. To soften the blow, she offered him a large estate and six thousand serfs. He agreed to give up his military position and retire to the countryside. Their break up was pricey for Catherine, and even more so for her troops—the peace talks with Turkey collapsed and war began again.

Now that her son Paul was nineteen years old something needed to be done with him. Privately, Catherine despaired about her unworthy heir. He was

Grand Duke Paul during his teenage years. *(The State Russian Museum.)*

much like Peter, the man he believed to be his father. He was obsessed with the military and hated Catherine. He often accused her of trying to kill him and was prone to fits of violence and even seizures.

Though she would not have welcomed the comparison, there were elements of Catherine's reign that resembled Elizabeth's. Catherine also had a male heir she considered unsuitable whom she planned to marry off in hopes he would produce children she could use to replace him. Just as Elizabeth had, Catherine turned to Frederick II for a suitable bride and, just as he had offered the obscure German princess Sophie all those years ago, Frederick now suggested the obscure German princess Wilhelmina. Accordingly, she was brought to Russia and examined. Both mother and son found her more than satisfactory, and she

Grand Duchess Natalia. *(The Romanov Gallery at the Winter Palace in St. Petersburg, Russia.)*

was put through the same period of study and conversion. Renamed Natalia, this lovely young woman married Paul on September 29, 1773, becoming the newest pawn in Catherine's game. Catherine waited anxiously for the signs of a grandchild. She would not have to wait as long as Elizabeth had.

Soon after Paul's wedding, Catherine received a distinguished visitor. Her long-time correspondent, sixty-year-old Denis Diderot, made the journey from Paris to St. Petersburg to pay his respects to his great benefactor—and perhaps encourage her to support more of his projects. Diderot's visit was greeted with enthusiasm by Catherine, until it became apparent that his exhortations and lectures were much more palatable when delivered in the mail than in person. The ideas and beliefs she had exclaimed over when she was biding her time waiting for Elizabeth to die now sounded somewhat foolish to the war-worn czarina. As she listened to the old man prattle on, the forty-four-year-old czarina smiled politely but seethed inside. For, even as Diderot was insisting on the importance of offering freedom to the serfs of Russia, Catherine was receiving news of a violent and dangerous serf rebellion.

The serfs of Russia lived, worked, and died in miserable conditions. They paid heavy taxes and working conditions in factories and mines were terrible. But, because the upper classes relied on serf labor for goods, services, and money, there was little sympathy for their causes or interest in reform. However, the serfs made up as much as ninety-five percent of the Russian population—any rebellion had the potential to be devastating.

An engraving depicting a serf's house in Russia during Catherine's rule. *(From Katerina die Zweite by Brucker.)*

Leader of the serf rebellion, Emelyan Pugachev.

The 1773 uprising began in a remote section of the Ural mountains when a man named Emelyan Pugachev began telling people he was Peter III returned from the grave, charged by God to bring justice to his long-suffering country.

The rebellion started in the eastern boundaries of the empire in Orenburg, a frontier town along the boundary between Europe and Asia. There mine workers had been threatening to strike for better working conditions and more pay. In the spring of 1773 Pugachev arrived in Orenburg with a ragtag band of followers. He ordered peasants to assert their independence: "You will no longer work for a lord and you will no longer pay taxes; if we find you toiling on behalf of another, we will massacre you all." His band of followers grew in size and began to gather up guns.

The revolt spread quickly across the countryside. By the time Pugachev's supporters reached the Volga River in northwestern Russia, they numbered over fifteen thousand. They were soon joined by thousands more who turned against their masters with the fury produced by generations of oppression. Rural soldiers in what had been sleepy outposts were unable to stop the slaughter of landlords, the rape and murder of their wives and children, or the burning of mansions. Pugachev offered bounties for each noble killed, each estate destroyed.

Catherine issued a proclamation declaring that Pugachev was an imposter and a traitor. She spread the word to the other European capitals that this was not a serious situation. But after six weeks of slaughter she could dissemble no longer. Though she wanted to focus on the ongoing war with Turkey, she wrote angrily of Pugachev, "I have been obliged to give my undivided attention to the affair."

In July, Pugachev and his ragtag army stormed Kazan, where the newly emerging industrial revolution had begun to take root. Regular army forces defeated the serfs, but only momentarily. The Russian commanders discovered that many of their troops did not want to fight against the rebels. For almost nine months, Pugachev evaded capture and his guerillas continued to inflict damage. Catherine was perhaps most annoyed that Pugachev was sometimes hailed as the reincarnation of Peter III. Her former husband had been vocally anti-Russian and now this maniac in front of an army of serfs was claiming him as an inspiration. She had done more for Russia than Peter ever had or would if he had lived. Now, in death, he had become a hero to her ungrateful people.

Pugachev was finally captured in September 1774, arrested, tried, and found guilty of treason. In an act of mercy, Catherine ordered that his head be cut off before his body was torn into pieces. Pugachev's head was displayed on a pole in Moscow and his accomplices tortured and killed.

German glass commemorating Russia's victory over the Turks in 1774.

Once Pugachev was stopped, Catherine did nothing to alleviate the problems that had given rise to the rebellion. She did not even try to stop the cruel retribution landlords meted out. In many ways, the Pugachev revolt marked the end of Catherine the reformer. She had grown frustrated at the hidebound Russian traditions. It seemed that she was locked into a calcified system that could not change. She had once believed the serfs of Russia should be freed. Now they had risen in bloody, destructive revolt, while Russia was engaged in a war with Turkey. Maybe they did not deserve to be free? A more tired and cynical Catherine began to wonder if the Enlightenment philosophy she so admired could be applied to the Russian system. She had once been committed to opening up Russia, to bringing the more liberal ideas of the west to her adopted and beloved country. But now she became a vocal, even strident, advocate of the oppressive class system.

By July 1774, the Russians had finally achieved a clear-cut victory over the Turks. The Black Sea was open to Russian commerce. Catherine staged a lavish peace ceremony in Moscow to honor the victorious Russian officers. A year later, another round of celebrations was held in honor of the peace treaty that had been signed with the Turks. The agreement extended the Russian empire to the northern shores of the Black Sea, including land in the Caucasus Mountains in southwestern Russia and along the shores of the Russian boundary with eastern Turkey. Russian merchants were granted the right to pass through the Dardenelles. The Turks also agreed to respect the independence of the Crimea, the fertile peninsula of almost ten thousand square miles that extended into the Black Sea. The end of the war was a clear declaration to the rest of Europe that Russia would play an important part in future geographical and political questions in the region—and that Catherine was a powerful political and military leader.

After six years of war, Catherine boasted that "at the end of each one [war] she [Russia] seems to emerge more flourishing than before." Although the treasury was nearly empty she considered the nation to be wealthy because of the potential wealth in the Siberian mines and the quarries of the Urals, the churches and palaces, and her collections of paintings and sculpture. She wrote proudly, "every Russian peasant has always a chicken ready for the pot."

In this painting, the new king of France, Louis XVI, is being received by the Knights of the Order of Saint Espirit. The French court had long been characterized by the excess and pagentry depicted here. *(Courtesy of Art Resource.)*

1774 brought Catherine happy news: Louis XV, king of France, was dead. She had long been hostile to the French government, largely because they had refused to come to her aid when she was making her bid for the throne. Now that Louis XV was dead, her stance softened quite a bit. She was pleased to see Louis XVI ascend to power and relations between the two countries improved immensely.

Bored by her latest lover, one selected for his physical, not mental, attributes, Catherine renewed her acquaintance with Gregory Potemkin. Orlov's jealousy of the young man had resulted in his exile years before. Now, the letters she sent him were received warmly. After several exchanges, Potemkin requested Catherine's permission to leave his post

Catherine and her lifelong confidant, Gregory Potemkin.

in the army and enter a monastery—he could not bear the thought of living in the world without her love, he said. Catherine, smitten, had him transferred to St. Petersburg.

This began the most intimate and fulfilling relationship of Catherine's life. Potemkin was a mature man—thirty-five to her forty-five years old. He was a seasoned, scarred warrior (he lost his left eye in a fight) who was savvy about the ways of government and diplomacy. She was at the height of her power and confidence as a ruler, and the two made an excellent pair.

Catherine entrusted Potemkin with many responsibilities in her government, a trust he took seriously and handled well. Unlike the hotheaded and unruly Orlov, Potemkin had a stabilizing effect on the czarina. It is possible they may have even secretly married—from the end of 1774 on, her surviving letters to him use the words husband and wife freely.

Potemkin worked closely with Catherine on matters of state both domestic and international. He proved to be an extraordinary statesman with vast knowledge of the southern provinces and their inhabitants. Catherine grew dependent on his presence, nagging him when he was off on other business and constantly begging for expressions of his love. Someone said about the couple, "They love each other for they are exactly alike," referring to their mutual lust for power and ambition.

Because Potemkin and Catherine were so well suited emotionally and intellectually, their relationship was able to survive the eventual cooling of their affair. When the flames of their passion died down after about two years, Potemkin took it upon himself to introduce the czarina to another attractive young man—one with more looks than brains. Cleverly, Potemkin realized that if he could keep Catherine supplied with pretty but empty-headed boyfriends she would not have reason to replace him. He would retain his power and prestige in the government instead of suffering ignominious exile the way Orlov had. As these handsome young men passed through the court, Catherine and her aides developed a processing system to determine their suitability. Each was first discreetly introduced to the czarina in a public setting. If she approved of the selection, the young man was taken for a thorough doctor's exam. Once he passed that, he was gently but firmly quizzed about a variety of subjects by one of Catherine's ladies-in-waiting. Her job was to make sure there was nothing overtly objectionable about his intellect. The next test was a more intimate one, to ensure he would be capable in the bedroom. Through this procedure, Peter Zavadovsky, Simon Zorich, Ivan Rimsky-Korsakov, and more were brought to Catherine's court and treated, for a time, like princes. They were showered with gifts and money and handsomely rewarded when their services were no longer required. And Potemkin watched over them all with his one good eye.

7

Enlightened Despot

In April of 1776, Paul's wife Natalia gave birth to a stillborn child. Her pregnancy had created great excitement. Catherine was particularly pleased at the prospect of having a child she could raise, much as Elizabeth had raised Paul—but hopefully with better results—to be czar. The baby's death was a crushing disappointment. Then the tragedy was compounded when Natalia died a few days later. Paul was overcome by grief and the whole court went into mourning—except, that is, for Catherine. The czarina had become unimpressed by her daughter-in-law, who had been an ambitious woman Catherine was convinced was plotting to have Paul crowned czar. Catherine had also long known about the affair Natalia had been conducting with Paul's best friend; a circumstance she had tolerated only because she longed for a grandchild.

Natalia was hardly buried before Catherine began to look for another wife for her son. The grieving Paul resisted the idea of marrying again, so Catherine revealed Natalia's affair. Paul was devastated by the revelation but it had the effect Catherine desired: he gave up mourning his wife and child and submitted to her plans for another marriage. By midsummer, Frederick II had provided another German princess and Paul was engaged to sixteen-year-old Sophia Dorothea. Catherine rushed the plans for the wedding. She wanted heirs to the throne, and she wanted them right away. She hurried the bride's conversion to Orthodoxy, saying, "The princess' religious instruction should not take more than a fortnight. Conviction will come later." Sophia Dorothea became Maria Feodorovna and the Grand Duchess of Russia less than a year after her successor was buried.

Maria Feodorovna, Paul's second wife, in a portrait done by Lampi.

Paul's behavior was becoming more and more objectionable to his mother. She was continually disappointed to see how much his interests and personality resembled Peter's. Paul's military obsession frustrated Catherine. Now he seemed little more than a spoiled, bitter child. But Catherine was very pleased with Paul's new wife, who dutifully began producing children almost right away.

Catherine celebrated extravagantly the birth of her first grandson, Grand Duke Alexander Pavlovich. The final event of the celebration was a banquet that a British ambassador said was characterized by "magnificence and good taste which surpassed anything that can be conceived. The dessert at supper was set out with jewels valued at over two million pounds sterling." The site of the feast, the Winter Palace, had become a treasure house of art with rare tapestries, antique statues, and exquisite furniture.

Once again, Catherine's actions came to mirror those of the woman she had both loved and hated—the Czarina Elizabeth. It had hurt Catherine deeply to have her children taken from her at their births, yet she did not think twice about doing the same to Maria and Paul. Catherine raised Alexander as if he was her own son—and she did the same with his brother Constantine, born soon after. She was determined that these boys would grow up to rule. Alexander would succeed her to the throne of Russia; Constantine was named in honor of the city she hoped to conquer and make him the ruler of some day. Maria and Paul would go on to have ten children. Catherine let them keep and raise the girls, but took charge of the boys herself. This earned her son and daughter-in-law's enmity, just as Elizabeth had earned hers.

At age fifty, Catherine still had the regal posture, gracious smile, and sparkling blue eyes she had as the little princess from Zerbst. But she had grown quite stout and her hair was almost totally gray. In culture as well as in other aspects of Russian life, Catherine continued to try to bridge the gulf between Russia and Europe. She acquired new collections of art, including some magnificent paintings by Peter Paul Rubens and a Sir Anthony Vandyke masterpiece. She tried to induce European artists to work in Russia.

Catherine sponsored the Academy of Science, which also supported artists, and furnished her palaces with a magnificent assortment of mirrors, furniture, china, tapestries, and wall hangings. One of her palaces included a Chinese pavilion and sophisticated replicas of the ice hills and toboggan slides found in amusement parks. She kept enormous greenhouses full of fruits from Russia and all over the world. In St. Petersburg she had canals lined with granite slabs which gave new beauty and convenience to the Neva River. She wrote six plays in less than two years—preferring comedies to tragedies and happy endings to sad ones. Though she was not an especially talented playwright, she threw herself into the effort as tirelessly as she did everything else. Although she was tone-deaf, Catherine subsidized orchestras.

Under Catherine's control, Russia had become a major player in Europe—socially, economically, and most significantly, politically. Catherine was now one of the powerful rulers other countries turned to for help or approval. Her troops were solicited by both the British and the Americans during the American Revolution, but Catherine did not want

Catherine the Great with her court on the steps of a palace just outside of St. Petersburg. *(Courtesy of Art Resource.)*

to appease either side by offering military support. She decided to rest her army, which was still recovering from the Pugachev rebellion, and focus on maintaining her own borders.

When the Elector of Bavaria, Maximilian Joseph, died in 1777, his death offered Austria the opportunity it had long been waiting for to expand its territory. Without a strong leader, Bavaria should fall easily to Austria's advances. Bavaria and Austria were predominantly Catholic, while Prussia was Lutheran. Emperor Joseph II of Austria was opposed by his great enemy, Frederick the II of Prussia, who did not want to see Austria increase its size or influence in Germany.

In April of 1778, Frederick II declared war on Austria.

Both sides appealed to Catherine for support and she was faced with one of her most difficult diplomatic decisions. She had been able to partition Poland because she had support from both Prussia and Austria. There was the danger that if she offended either of the emperors he would side with the Turks and throw Russia into a two-front war. After much contemplation, Catherine ventured an opinion. In the most diplomatic terms possible, she suggested to Joseph that Austria's claims on Bavaria were not legitimate. Catherine's carefully worded letter was enough to force Joseph to do as she suggested. Prussia and Austria signed a peace treaty less than a year after war began and Bavaria was left intact.

After the tension about Bavaria was over, Catherine began to consider making Russia a neutral power. It was diffi-cult for a country to maintain neutrality— Russia would find itself goaded and pressured by one or both sides of a con-flict. It was not un-common for warring parties to try to trick neutral countries into

Frederick II of Prussia.

coming to their aid. One of the easiest ways of doing so was on the high seas—for example, a French ship might hoist a Spanish flag and dress its sailors in the Spanish uniform then attack ships belonging to a neutral country. When the reports of Spanish piracy reached the ship's home port, France would hope that country would throw in on its side. Catherine was determined to avoid this kind of trickery—not only was it a threat to international diplomacy but it made shipping more dangerous and expensive.

Catherine drew up a document entitled "Declaration of Maritime Neutrality" which she hoped would effectively end this sort of piracy. The declaration made it illegal for warring parties to interfere with the commerce of neutral countries. A simple plan, it was hailed across Europe as revolutionary in its brilliance. The only country displeased by Catherine's declaration was Great Britain, whose power resided in its having the largest and most powerful navy in the world. Great Britain's cool reception had the unintended consequence of pushing Catherine's allegiances even closer to France, who had recently decided to intervene on the side of the colonists fighting the British in North America.

Voltaire died in 1778. Catherine was deeply moved by his passing—though they had never met, his correspondence and unflagging support of her reforms had been extremely important to her. In many ways, it was Voltaire who made Catherine famous in Europe. He wrote poetry that sang her praises and presented her to literate Europe as an enlightened ruler. Catherine ordered an enormous tomb built in his honor and arranged to purchase his private library.

Joseph II of Austria. *(Courtesy of Art Resource.)*

Emperor Joseph II of Austria was intrigued by the stories about Catherine. Although she had taken Frederick II's side in the Bavarian conflict, Joseph was interested in Catherine and wrote suggesting they meet. It was an unusual offer but

Catherine accepted it. Their meeting was a productive one for both—each knew the other had designs on conquering more of Europe. Privately they agreed on a mutual support system if it became necessary for either country to defend itself from Sweden, Turkey, Prussia or any other enemy. Because both rulers were anxious to pick off pieces of the Turkish empire, they reached an agreement to avoid interfering with the one another's claims. Austria was welcome to try to annex Serbia, Bosnia, and Herzegovina in the Balkans, while Russia was free to try to take Constantinople and the Crimea. The risk of another war against the Turks in the Crimea had been on Catherine's mind for several years. She believed Russia could never be at peace with the Turks as long they supported anti-Russian rebels in the Crimea. Furthermore, she continued to dream of recapturing Constantinople before she died.

It would be foolish to put too much trust in Austria, however. Catherine did not trust Joseph completely, but she was pleased that he had sought her out. It served the purpose of putting Frederick II on notice. Anxious about any pact between Russia and his archenemy Austria, the Prussian emperor sent his best diplomats to Catherine's court in an attempt to come between her and Joseph. But Catherine had chosen her side, for better or for worse, and the Russian-Austrian alliance grew stronger.

Catherine's great desire to see her grandson Constantine rule in the city he was named for was no secret in her court. Paul realized that his mother hoped to find a way to cut him out of the line of succession. He had long been upset that he had not been given the throne at the age of eighteen, as many people believed he should have. He grew bitter, hanging around in the background, watching his mother manipulate the most powerful rulers in Europe. Paul spoke openly about the changes he would make once Catherine's rule was over. He planned to undo everything she had worked so hard to accomplish. Catherine's spies kept her informed about her son's injudicious comments, which only strengthened her conviction that he must not gain her throne. To find some measure of peace, she tricked Paul and his wife into taking a tour of Europe. But the plan backfired; reports of Paul's obnoxious behavior and outrageous boasting poured into St. Petersburg.

In an effort to ensure her grandsons would not grow up to be like their father, Catherine took complete control over all aspects of their lives. She insisted they be bathed only in cold water and not be coddled in any way—she wanted them to grow up strong, like the brave Russian soldiers she admired. She hired a tutor who promised he could make men

Catherine's beloved grandsons, Alexander and Constantine.

of them. Catherine supervised their course of study, demanding that her grandsons be taught that lying was wrong and that love and respect for nature and their subjects was right. In a twist, their tutor was an avowed republican—a believer in the power and intellect of the people. As Catherine aged, she became more and more anti-republican. She was still considered an enlightened ruler outside of Russia, but in her own country Catherine was clearly an autocrat.

The Crimea, the focus of her expansion plans, had been under Russian control in everything but name until Gregory Potemkin negotiated with Turkey to have the area formally ceded to Russia. Catherine was so pleased with her former lover's success that she made him a prince. He retained the title of Field Marshall and ruled over the Crimea with a careful hand. He also supervised the military and was popular for the many reforms he began. He forbade the whipping of recruits, issued new and comfortable uniforms, and promoted personal hygiene. He respected religious creeds and his battalions were formed according to race and nationality—Potemkin's army even had a battalion made up entirely of Jews.

Potemkin had also continued in his role as Catherine's procurer of lovers. One of the young men he brought to her made the mistake of disrespecting his benefactor. He whispered to Catherine that Potemkin was skimming money from state funds for his own personal use. When Potemkin heard these accusations, he flew into a rage and marched across Russia to confront the czarina himself. He told her she must choose between him and her new plaything.

Catherine, no fool, ordered her consort to leave the palace immediately. She did not doubt that the rumors were true, but a few rubles were a small price to pay for the loyalty and talents of a man such as Potemkin.

Catherine's success was in part due to the people she sur-

Princess Dashkova was sent into exile under Paul's rule. After Paul's death, Alexander I allowed her to return to St. Petersburg. *(The Hermitage Museum.)*

rounded herself with. Though she made some personnel mistakes, mainly by giving her lovers too much political power, she also made some excellent decisions. One such decision was to appoint the headstrong and passionate Princess Dashkova to head the Russian Academy. Though the princess initially rejected the position, Catherine refused to take no for an answer. In the end, Dashkova's Academy was a triumph. She modeled her work on the French Academy and oversaw the creation of the first-ever dictionary of the Russian language. She worked to standardize spelling and grammar and was a supporter of the fledgling Russian art community. After years of deferring to their European counterparts, Russian artists finally began to make their own mark.

In June of 1784, Catherine's latest lover, Alexander Lanskoy, her "man of gold," contracted diphtheria and died. Catherine was distraught. She allowed no one in her rooms for days, not even her beloved grandchildren. Only Potemkin, summoned to the court, could reach her. Under his compassionate hand, she was finally brought back into the world. Even a czarina had feelings—even a czarina could mourn. But Catherine the Great of Russia could not abandon her throne.

After a summer in seclusion, Catherine returned to the Hermitage and tried to begin a new life. She was unable to bring herself to entertain, and it was February 1786 before she moved back to the Winter Palace. Potemkin kept suggesting a new lover. Thirty-one-year-old Alexis Yermolov appealed to her—she liked his dog-like devotion and honesty: "I have found a friend who is very capable and very worthy of the name," she wrote. After Yermolov came twenty-six-year-old Alexander Mamonov. The fifty-seven-year-old czarina was still a passionate woman and continued to enjoy the parade of young men through her court.

8

Potemkin Village

Catherine the Great's rule was successful in many ways. She took a backward and isolated country and opened it to European influences while, at the same time, encouraging a uniquely Russian culture to bloom. She had done her best to reform and codify the bizarre and archaic Russian legal system. Her reputation as an enlightened leader was further enhanced by her tolerance of various religions. Catherine's own religious conversion and her study of the Enlightenment philosophers left her open to the idea of a secular state. She accepted Orthodox, Roman Catholic, Lutheran, Jewish, and Muslim believers—although she was not personally tolerant of Jews. Her prejudice came not from religion but from her belief that Jews had an unfair advantage in business. Jews had been driven into commerce and money lending to a great degree because of restrictions that barred them from most artisan professions. This left only a few occupations, including selling wares and lending money, open to them. At one point, in order to protect Moscow's merchants from what she perceived as unfair trade practices, Catherine ordered a so-called Pale of Settlement that restricted the areas in which Jews could live around the city.

To foreign travelers, St. Petersburg was a striking example of growth and prosperity. Handsome buildings, bustling wharves, new factories, and the elegance of the court created an image of undiminished wealth and luxury. Like most images, the reality was more complicated. One social problem, for example, was created by the large number of serfs who managed to escape from their masters hoping to become laborers in the city. Most of these men could not find permanent employment and, afraid or unwilling to return to their life of servitude, became roaming highwaymen or beggars. Still, St. Petersburg was cosmopolitan and exciting. Foreign diplomats assigned to Catherine's court were usually pleasantly surprised.

In January of 1787, Catherine took her first major trip since becoming czarina. She was proud of the recently acquired Crimea and wanted very much to visit it. Potemkin had sent her letters full of news about the changes he had made to the area. She planned a grand trip in honor of her twenty-fifth year on the throne and invited along guests from Austria, France, and even England. The journey would be a chance to show off the vastness and glory of Russia to the ambassadors.

With much pomp and ceremony, the travelers set out in

fourteen coaches, each pulled by eight or ten horses. Behind those comfortable conveyances came more than one hundred sleighs drawn by over five hundred horses. The temperature when they set out was seventeen degrees below zero and the travelers wore bearskins over their precious furs. They traveled ten hours a day, yet seemed to make little progress. Outside of a few scattered towns, Russia seemed to be nothing but a broad expanse of snow. Potemkin was in charge of most of the details of their trip. In order to guide the sleds across the featureless winter landscape

Catherine dressed in travel clothes for her trip to the Crimea.

he had ordered bonfires built along the route to signal the drivers. Those great fires, visible for miles in every direction, were kept burning twenty-four hours a day until Catherine's train swept by.

Finally, after a month of this travel, the party reached Kiev. They would wait out the winter there and then proceed down the Dnieper River when spring came. The company was a lively one—although Catherine still insisted there be neither foul language nor racy stories. In addition to the cosmopolitan and amusing French ambassador, Comte Louis Philippe de Ségur, they were joined by the Belgian-born Prince Charles de Ligne, confidante of Joseph II of Austria. The fifty-year-old de Ligne was charming and possessed a thorough knowledge of world affairs. He was as enchanted by Catherine as she was by him—he found her modest lifestyle appealing. He wrote home that he was fascinated "to see the conqueror of the Turks tending her flowers, the legislator of the greatest of empires sowing her own lawns, her very simplicity contrasting with the splendor of her exploits." Catherine said in turn that he was "the pleasantest company and the easiest person to live with that I have ever met." She was so relaxed on this trip that de Ségur was able to coax her into signing a favorable trade treaty with France.

When spring came, Potemkin arranged for seven enormous ships to take the main members of Catherine's party down the Dnieper River, which flowed southwest to the Black Sea. The journey would take them thousands of miles through steppes and deserts, parts of which were uninhabited. Behind the seven main ships came a flotilla of sixty-three more, manned by three thousand oarsmen. Many of those laborers were convicts literally chained to their oars.

Potemkin spared no effort or expense to make the czarina's journey a pleasant one. Where it was necessary, he had workers dig furiously to widen the river to ease the ships' passing. There were rumors that he hid ugly houses behind quickly built facades of cheap wood. Others said there were no ugly houses to hide but that Potemkin ordered facades built to represent entire villages that did not exist. Some people believe Potemkin had soldiers dressed as peasants working in these villages as the boats went by—once they were out of sight, the soldiers would mount their horses and gallop ahead to their next imaginary home. As a result of

Potemkin showing Catherine an apparently prosperous village along the Dnieper.

these rumors, the phrase "Potemkin village" has come to refer to something that is a sham.

As the party continued its travel, visitors joined and departed. One temporary visitor was the king of Poland, Catherine's old lover Stanislas Poniatowski. They had been separated for twenty-eight years, during which time Poniatowski had endured danger and abuse for his constant obedience to her wishes. She had taken and discarded many lovers since they last saw each other, but he had remained faithful to the idea that she was the only woman he had ever loved. It was a tremendous disappointment to him that Catherine allowed her latest boyfriend to sit in on their reunion, and that she hardly listened when he spoke or spoke to him at all. Poniatowski had allowed her to shape the course of his entire life—she had made him a king and then asked him to betray his country—and now she would not repay him with so much as a smile. Catherine was not sorry to see the now mopey old man go, and was even happier to see the witty and amusing Joseph II take his place. Even diplomatic tensions between France and England were not allowed to mar the trip. Catherine made light of having the two ambassadors from the warring countries in such close quarters by forcing them to share a tent one night. The tent had only one table, so the ambassadors had to sit facing each other, just inches apart, as each one worked on his top-secret report. The rest of the travelers found the situation hilarious.

Once they reached the Crimea, Catherine insisted on entering surrounded by a guard of native troops, not Russians. She wanted to show the inhabitants that she came in peace. Though some in her entourage were uncomfortable, Catherine smiled serenely as twelve hundred armed Tatars enveloped their carriages and escorted them into the city. Catherine's trust in these warriors was complete, and in return for their service she promised to protect their religion and culture. It was highly unusual for a Muslim nation to peacefully receive a Christian ruler, and a woman at that, but Catherine's blend of firmness and compassion made the transition easy.

Catherine's headquarters in the Crimea was a former palace carefully restored by an architect commissioned by Potemkin. Marble fountains, secret gardens, and glittering illumination created a fairy-tale like setting. The city bazaars bustled all day and night; lights glorified the banquets, fireworks blazed, and singers and dancers from every province performed for the assembled dignitaries.

The reality of the Potemkin villages they passed on their way into the Crimea may have been in doubt, but there was no way Potemkin could have faked the splendor of the port city Sevastopol: there were churches, hospitals, and schools, that had all been built in just three years. Catherine thanked her loyal friend publicly, comparing the work he had done to the modernization of Russia begun by her other hero, Peter the Great. After twenty-five years on the Russian throne, Catherine was beginning to imagine she might accomplish all she had hoped for.

Taking advantage of Sevastopol's prominent place on the shores of the Black Sea, Potemkin put on a fearsome display of Russia's military prowess. There he deployed his fleet of sixteen man-of-wars and twenty-four battle ships, all in formation, dipping their flags and firing their guns in a royal salute. Catherine was thrilled, but again some of the men in her entourage were uncomfortable. They knew that Potemkin's show of military prowess was not just for Catherine's benefit but for the eyes and ears of the Turks just across the Black Sea. Catherine had not put aside her plan to see Constantine rule over Constantinople. Joseph II of Austria warned Catherine to handle the Turks carefully. The French ambassador echoed his sentiment, but Catherine laughed at them both.

What Catherine might not have quite realized was how her increasing power had made her seem more dangerous. Countries that would have, and did, support her just five or ten years ago were now rethinking their positions. Though the Turks had few friends in Europe, leaders were beginning to think that a weak Turkey might be preferable to a powerful Russia. Behind Catherine's back, the leaders of Europe worked to inflame the Turks against her. If her display of military might at Sevastopol made the Turks angry, Europe's whispers encouraged them to retaliate.

In August 1787, Turkey took the official first step towards reopening the hostilities between the two nations when they demanded the return of the Crimea. Catherine told her ambassador to say no. He was promptly arrested and put in a Turkish jail and once again Russia and Turkey were at war. England and Prussia sided with Turkey, France declared itself neutral, and Joseph II of Austria agreed to fight with Catherine.

Although it was obvious that Russian troops were not prepared for war, Catherine confidently proclaimed: "in two weeks all troops can be in place." She refused to acknowledge that famine and drought had weakened the Russians both physically and morally. To make matters worse, the Russian troops were scattered all over the country. The Turks, by contrast, were rested and ready to fight. They saw this as a holy war to protect Islam, and were anxious to take on the hated Russia.

Catherine appointed Potemkin supreme commander, promoting him over those leaders who had been working with the military while Potemkin was preparing Russia for Catherine's trip. Now he faced another challenge. He had to repair a fleet that had been badly battered in a storm, build a large number of other boats to carry men to the enemy, rebuild sixteen infantry battalions and ten thousand cavalry, supply the artillery with oxen as well as food, and create a strong military presence.

Three months after the war started, it was obvious Potemkin was not up to the task. He did a good job of preparing the army to fight, but for whatever reason he was reluctant to actually commit his troops to battle. Catherine sent a flurry of letters from St. Petersburg urging her old friend and lover to proceed. He replied listlessly and appeared to be erratic. For the first time, Catherine began to worry.

When John Paul Jones, an American hero in the Revolutionary War, appeared in Russia to offer his services, Catherine made him a rear admiral attached to the Baltic

John Paul Jones.

fleet. Jones served under Potemkin with distinction. He introduced discipline and order into his squadron and led the fleet to victory in battle. He was brave, sneaking out in a rowboat under the cover of darkness in order to spy on the Turkish fleet. But after a nasty conflict between the capable Jones and the now inert Potemkin, Catherine had to dismiss him from her service.

For Catherine the end of 1788 and January of 1789 was a difficult period. For several months, she had suffered colic, pains in her sides and back, and could not sleep for worrying about Potemkin. In June 1788, the Swedish king Gustavus III—with the support of Germany and England—took advantage of Russia's war with Turkey to attack from the west. Swedish troops invaded the Russian mainland and were within a few days' march of St. Petersburg when problems back home in Sweden forced Gustavus to withdraw his soldiers.

The Swedish reprieve was a tremendous boon for the Russians. Potemkin finally gathered himself together and the Russian armies began winning victories on every front—

although the losses were tremendous and the suffering intense. In one battle, a total of nearly eighty thousand soldiers were killed. The help Catherine had hoped to receive from Joseph II did not come. His soldiers were busy stopping an uprising in the Netherlands. Russian forces were stretched even thinner when the Swedes renewed their attack.

As 1789 began, Catherine held out hope that France would intervene to help mediate a peace for Russia and Turkey. Catherine's hopes were dashed when the news arrived about the French revolution. The French monarchy had long struggled with several intractable problems, including an antiquated taxation system, a powerful Catholic clergy, and nobles who resisted any effort to reform. The middle class and peasants paid the vast majority of the taxes and enjoyed few of the benefits.

The crisis in France was brought on by an economic collapse. Due in part to the money that had been spent helping the Americans defeat Great Britain, the treasury was empty by 1789. King Louis XVI had no choice but to call the Estates General, the seldom used national assembly. Unable to reach an agreement, the Estates General collapsed and was replaced by a more radical National Assembly, which demanded major political and economic reforms. When the crown resisted, mobs took to the streets of Paris and stormed the hated Bastille, a prison, and tore it apart stone by stone. Peasants and workers long unhappy with the rule of Louis XVI turned against him and the other aristocrats in a bloody and violent uprising. They established a new, republican, government and imprisoned those responsible for the old one. Many of the former French rulers, including the king and the queen, were eventually beheaded.

Catherine was shocked and furious at the events in France. She had no sympathy for the rebels. She came to realize that some of her favorite philosophers, especially Voltaire, were partly responsible for spreading the ideas of freedom and republicanism that inspired the revolt. She felt betrayed and angry. Many European governments felt threatened by the revolution in France. They worried republican sentiment could spread to their people. Catherine took preemptive measures. She began to persecute dissidents more harshly, restricted free speech and the press, and imprisoned anyone suspected of criticizing the Russian government.

Catherine exiled Alexander Radishchev, the author of *A Journey from St. Petersburg to Moscow*, which was highly critical of the horrors of serfdom and the widespread corruption in Russia. Though she tried, she was not able to confiscate all copies of the book. Public reaction to *A Journey from St. Petersburg to Moscow* was overwhelmingly favorable and copies were sold under the counter. Luckily for Catherine, her country was too big and its population too decentralized and illiterate for revolutionary spirit to catch hold. The French ambassador who had so delighted the czarina, de Ségur, asked her permission to return home to find out what had become of his wife and family. Catherine was very sorry to see him go and could not resist warning him that if, as she feared, he embraced republican ideals upon his return to France, they could never speak again. De Ségur was flattered but undeterred. Despite Catherine's hatred of the French revolution, she continued to pay for the services of her grandsons' tutor, an avowed republican. She wanted the boys to grow up educated and worldly young men—but she would later regret her choice of educators.

1790 brought more bad news—Emperor Joseph II of Austria died. His brother Leopold, who was as anti-Russian as his brother had been pro, succeeded him. Frederick II of Prussia had also retired four years earlier and left his throne in the hands of his repellent nephew, Frederick William II. Leopold and Frederick William made plans to join forces, a move that would deprive Catherine of her most important support. Leopold also made plans to pull Austria out of the war with Turkey.

Then the Russian fleet suffered a tremendous defeat at the hands of the Swedes. Catherine's fleet commander appeared before her to beg for his dismissal. He tried to return all his medals, saying that he had not proven himself worthy of wearing them. She told the distraught officer that he was hardly the first one to suffer a defeat, and that the point was to continue to try—not to give up. She told him to return to his ships and to earn his medals back.

In June, Russia scored a victory over the Swedish fleet in the gulf of Vyborg near the Russian-Finnish border. The tide of the war seemed to be turning, but it was internal dissension in Sweden that brought hostilities to an end. The king did not have the backing of his nobility and could no longer sustain a fight. Abruptly, in August 1790, the Rus-

Plato Zubov, one of Catherine's lovers.

sians and Swedes signed a peace treaty. The terms were such that neither country could claim victory—the Russian-Swedish borders were unchanged. Still, Catherine was pleased to at last devote all of her troops to war with Turkey.

At home in St. Petersburg, Catherine, sixty, took a new lover. Twenty-two-year-old Plato Zubov replaced Alexander Mamonov, who had been having a clandestine affair with one of her ladies-in-waiting. When she realized Mamonov's deception she was privately outraged that he had dared to defy her, but publicly she was kind to the couple, even blessing their marriage ceremony. She gave them an estate in the country. Within a few weeks, Mamonov was writing to Catherine, begging to be allowed back at the court. He swore he loved her and could not live without her, but Catherine may have suspected that what he really missed was the excitement and power he had enjoyed in her court. She ignored his letters and consoled herself with Zubov.

Perhaps because of Mamonov's deception Catherine wanted to tie Zubov to her more tightly. She showered the young man with gifts and allowed him enormous power in her court. Potemkin heard the news and was furious. He was jealous because Zubov was not under his control as so many of her previous lovers had been, but he also worried that the headstrong youngster could be a dangerous influence on Catherine. He left the Crimea and traveled to St. Petersburg to assess the situation.

Before he arrived in court, Potemkin's aides warned him that Catherine was in poor health and that she had become irritable and moody. She was more obese than ever and suffered from circulation problems; her legs were so swollen she had problems walking. She adamantly refused to see a doctor or to take medicine and relied on steam baths, walks when she was able, and a daily dose of pepper and Malaga wine. Some people in her court worried that Catherine's physical weakness and distress prevented her from fulfilling her duties. The aides told Potemkin that in view of Catherine's health, it was especially important that he seize control before Zubov could make any more inroads. Despite the fact that he had suffered two bouts of malaria in the past years, Potemkin resolved to save his czarina and her country.

Arriving in St. Petersburg, Potemkin was greeted by the most extravagant welcome ever seen in Russia. Nobles and members of the court competed to see who could put on the most lavish banquets, the most exciting performances, and the most thrilling entertainment. This was more upsetting than gratifying. Potemkin knew that the treasury was very low. The rate of exchange dropped daily, and there was scarcely any money in circulation.

Catherine attended many of these affairs, smiling all the while, even though she could walk only with great difficulty. Her obesity forced her to use ramps instead of stairs and to sit on two chairs in the theater. Zubov was always at her side, attending to her every need—on the outside he was obsequious, but on the inside, Potemkin believed, he was scheming for power.

The biggest celebration of all was for Catherine's sixty-second birthday. Wine spouted from fountains, barrels of roasted meat and hot pies were available to all, and Catherine rode through the square nodding and smiling to the crowds turned out to see her. The winter garden was full of orange and myrtle groves and exotic birds. Mirrors and statues filled every nook and cranny. The trunk of a golden elephant studded with emeralds was fitted with a device that called the guests to dinner.

Potemkin's trip was not a success. Catherine ignored his warnings about Zubov and continued to spoil her new favorite. Potemkin could see that her health was in decline, but there was little he could do. After a decent period, Catherine asked him to return to the Crimea and begin peace talks with the Turks. Potemkin dared not refuse the czarina. His coach had barely passed outside St. Petersburg when he began to feel ill. He asked the coachman to stop. "I'm dying," he said. "There is no point in going any further. I want to die on the ground." He struggled out of the carriage and sprawled on the dirt of his country. An hour later, Potemkin was dead.

The news of his death shocked Catherine deeply. She had come to count on Potemkin to take care of the southern part of Russia as if he was her own right hand. She was so overcome with grief, she could hardly move. She repeated over and over the question, "Whom shall I rely on now?"

9

The Future is the Past

The news of Potemkin's death seemed to sap Catherine of her strength. She insisted a peace treaty with Turkey be signed immediately, regardless of the terms. In her rush for resolution, she gained only the territory between the Dnieper and the Dneister Rivers instead of the much larger territory that Potemkin had hoped for. Russia kept the Crimea and access to the Black Sea, but the Turks retained control over the Dardenelles, the main passage from the Black Sea to the Aegean. Without the Dardenelles, the Black Sea ports were useless. The treaty signed in January 1792 did not bring Catherine joy. The cost had been high both in men and materials, Potemkin was not there to celebrate with her, and she felt alone and nervous about the revolutionary turmoil in Europe.

The new Prussian emperor, Frederick William II, had

A political cartoon published in Britain in 1791 depicts the world's perception of Catherine's life-long quest for a Russian Constantinople.

been encouraging the Poles to revolt against Russian control. The Polish nobles formed a confederation that incorporated the ideals of the French Revolution. In May 1791 they created a new Polish constitution. This document posed an immediate threat to Russian control. Catherine sorely missed Potemkin, her military advisor and ruling partner for the last seventeen years.

In the end, Catherine fixed on the solution of partitioning Poland again. She would include Prussia in the plan, as she had before, to gain its cooperation. Frederick William shifted his loyalty, and, faced with the threat of Russian guns, Catherine and Frederick William forced Poniatowski to preside over a parliament that agreed to the partition. At that assembly, the Russian ambassador to Poland declared "the troops of her Imperial Majesty would occupy the lands of any deputy who opposed the will of the nation." Under the new plan, Russia gained over 250,000 square kilometers and over 3,000,000 citizens. King Poniatowski returned to his palace in Warsaw where he remained, ignored and despised by his former subjects.

Poland was now one-third of its original size with a population of fewer than 4,000,000 and an army of less than 15,000. But in April 1794, a young Polish army officer began a revolt aimed at Polish independence. Thaddeus Kosciusko's rebellion started in Krakow and spread to every town in the country. The Russians fought back by massacring women and children until the streets were filled with corpses. Catherine ignored the stories of brutality and cheered her soldiers on, promising her military leaders a share of confiscated property and peasants who would become serfs. In the bloodiest massacre of the conflict, the Russians finally put down the rebellion in October.

Flush with her victory and convinced that the Poles could not be trusted, Catherine proposed yet another partition of Poland that took effect in January 1795. With that treaty, Russia acquired even more territory and the Poles were forced to submit to Russian occupation. Catherine had succeeded in destroying Poland.

Her satisfaction with the ending of the Polish rebellion was tempered by another bout of ill health. Overcome by streptococcus that spread inflammation throughout her skin, she lay in bed for several weeks in November and December, scarcely able to eat or sleep. Her stress was made greater by the influx of French nobility seeking asylum from the bloody revolution. Catherine was disgusted by Louis XVI's acceptance of his subjects' revolt and ordered all things French removed from her court. Any refugees who wanted to remain in the country were made to sign a loyalty oath to Catherine.

Though her health continued to fail, Catherine kept a sharp eye on international diplomacy. She now had ten grandchildren and planned to use their marriages to strengthen Russian alliances abroad. When Gustavus III, the king of Sweden who had invaded Russia, died, he was succeeded by his son, Gustavus IV. Catherine proposed a marriage between Gustavus IV and her granddaughter Alexandra—a match she hoped would make Russia safe from invasion. The negotiations were thorny, but both sides eventually approved. Alexandra and Gustavus proved more than agreeable. Everything seemed to be going perfectly until the day of the betrothal ceremony. As Alexandra, Catherine, and the entire Russian court waited, Gustavus stood outside the hall reviewing the marriage contract. When he realized the contract allowed Alexandra to keep her Orthodox faith, he threw it to the floor and declared the wedding off. When a messenger brought her the word Alexandra fainted while a humiliated Catherine had to lie that Gustavus was ill. Despite further talks, the two sides could not be reconciled and a chance to bring Sweden and Russia together was missed.

Alexander's marriage was much more successful. As was customary, Catherine selected a German wife for her favorite grandson. She still planned to disinherit Paul and see the handsome, intelligent, and confident Alexander crowned in her place. Paul's behavior was more erratic than ever, and Catherine was certain he would have few supporters if he chose to challenge Alexander's claim. What she did not count on was that Alexander would refuse her throne.

Alexander's marriage took place on September 28, 1793. Not long after, Catherine took him aside to discuss his inheritance. She worried that he might be reluctant to supplant his father, but believed he could be made to see that it was in everyone's best interests. Much to Catherine's surprise, Alexander refused the throne altogether. Patiently, he told his stunned grandmother that he envisioned living a quiet life in the country, surrounded by

Princess Elizabeth, Alexander's wife, in a portrait by Monier.

his gardens and his children. He did not want to rule Russia—he preferred a life of contemplation and happiness. Catherine tried to get Panin, Alexander's tutor and friend, to side with her, but the old republican refused—he could not encourage the son to take what belonged to the father. Catherine was flabbergasted but made a concerted effort to handle the situation coolly. Finally, after much discussion and reasoning, she managed to convince Alexander that he could achieve his republican goals best if he had power—and that he could help his people more by preventing his father's rule.

In 1796, Alexander and his wife Elizabeth presented Catherine with a great grandson, Nicholas. But this birth brought Catherine only sadness as she wondered what would become of the boy she would not be there to raise. The sixty-seven-year-old czarina decided it was time to announce her choice of successor to the world. She set November 24, 1796 as the day she would reveal Alexander's destiny. Catherine wrote her intentions on a piece of paper, sealed it, and put it in a box on her desk. Then, in early November, Catherine the Great suffered a stroke. She never recovered and died on November 5, 1796.

News of Catherine's death spread quickly. Jubilant but wary, her son Paul rushed to the palace. Once it became clear no one planned to arrest him, he quickly had himself crowned czar. Alexander, who knew about the paper Catherine signed stating he should be her heir, said nothing. Paul ordered all of Catherine's private papers to be burned. Her body was clothed in silver silk brocade and placed in

This political cartoon depicts the unpopular Czar Paul I, wearing his Prussian military uniform.

a splendid bed in the throne room for public display. On December 2, she was interred at the Peter and Paul Cathedral beside her despised husband. At Catherine's funeral, the Austrian de Ligne exclaimed: "*Catherine le Grand* (I hope that Europe will confirm this name that I have given her), *Catherine le Grand* is no more. These words are frightful to pronounce!…The most brilliant star that illumined our hemisphere has just been extinguished."

Ten years before she died, Catherine had amused herself by writing her own epitaph. It reads:

> Here lies Catherine the Second…She went to Russia in the year 1744 to marry Peter III. At the age of fourteen she formed the threefold resolution to please her husband, Elizabeth, and the nation. She neglected nothing to accomplish this. Eighteen years of boredom and loneliness caused her to read many books. Having ascended the throne of Russia, she wished to do good and sought to procure for her subjects happiness, liberty and property. She pardoned readily and hated

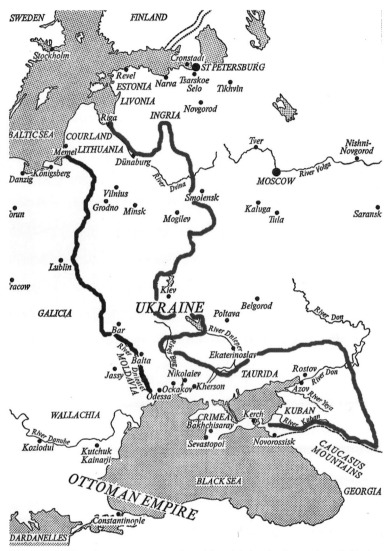

This map depicts the western expansion of Russia's border from when Catherine took power in 1762 (red) and when she died in 1796 (purple).

no one. Indulgent, easy to live with, possessed of a cheerful nature, a republican soul and a kind heart, she had friends. Work was easy for her, she enjoyed society and the arts.

Paul liberating the Polish prisoners, from a painting by Orlovsky.

As soon as he became Czar Paul I, Catherine's son began trying to undo all that his mother had done. He released the republicans and other revolutionaries from prison. He freed the leaders of the Polish revolt, including Kosciusko, who left for America. But perhaps most damaging, he tried to restore honor to his father. The Russian army was again dressed in Prussian uniforms and he began purging the military of Catherine's supporters.

Paul I reigned over an increasingly chaotic Russia as Europe slipped into a long series of wars against the French Republic. Unfortunately for Paul, he shared one more similarity with his father. After ruling four years he was assassinated by a group of conspirators and succeeded by his mysterious son Alexander. Though Alexander began his rule hoping to reform Russia, he eventually succumbed to the influence of a mystical sect of Christianity and was pushed off the throne by his son, Nicholas I.

In the coming years, a similar pattern was repeated. Russia's rulers came to power in violence and, despite their initial intentions to do well, the country continued to struggle through wars, crippled by the antiquated system of serfdom. The serfs were not freed until the end of the nineteenth century and, soon afterwards, the czars were overthrown for good. Joseph Stalin's rise to power meant the bloody legacy of the Russian rulers would continue.

Timeline

1729   Born in Stettin, Germany on May 2.

1744   Baptized in Russia, becomes Catherine; marries Peter.

1754   Paul is born.

1771   Czarina Elizabeth dies; Peter takes throne as Peter III.

1762   Catherine seizes throne, becomes Catherine II; Peter III dies.

1768   Russia declares war against Turkey.

1773   Pugachev revolt.

1774   War with Turkey ends.

1787   Turkey declares war on Russia.

1788   Sweden declares war on Russia.

1790   War with Sweden ends.

1791   War with Turkey ends.

1793   Partition of Poland.

1794   Another partition of Poland.

1796   Catherine dies on November 7.

RUSSIA BEFORE CATHERINE THE GREAT

400-600   Eastern Slavs migrate into what is now Ukraine and western Russia.

800-900   Swedish Vikings advance southwest into Novgorod and Kiev.

900-1240	Kiev is the center·of the Russian empire.
1200-1300	Mongols conquer Moscow and Kiev.
1300-1400	Poland captures territory in Belarus and Ukraine.
1328	Mongol Ivan Kalilta builds a kremlin (fortress) in Moscow.
1462-1500	Ivan III ends Mongol control of Russia.
1547-84	Ivan the Terrible is crowned czar of all Russia.
1584-1613	Anarchy and civil war prevail.
1613	Czar Mikhail Romanov restores stability.
1648	East Ukraine falls under Russian rule.
1682-1725	Peter the Great rules and introduces western ways.
1725-1727	Catherine I rules.
1727-1730	Peter II rules.
1730	Anna Ivanovna rules.
1733	Russia invades Poland.
1734	Ukraine comes under Russian control.
1737	Russians forced to evacuate Crimea.
1740	The infant Ivan VI ascends under the regency of Anna Leopoldovna.
1741	Elizabeth overthrows Ivan and takes throne; Sweden declares war on Russia.
1762	Death of Elizabeth; accession of Peter III.
1763	Peter overthrown: accession of Catherine II.

RUSSIA AFTER CATHERINE THE GREAT

1796	Paul I rules as military dictator.
1801	Paul is assassinated; Alexander I takes throne.
1812	Napoleon occupies Moscow, Muscovites set fire to city, Napoleon withdraws.
1825-1855	Decembrist rising crushed by Nicholas in 1825.
1855-1881	Alexander II liberates the serfs, is assassinated
1881-94	Alexander III leads rapid industrialization.

1894-1917	Nicholas II unable to quell revolution.
1898	Social Democratic party created under Vladimir Lenin.
1905	Bloody Sunday—hundreds of protesters are killed.
1914	Russia enters World War I against Germany.
1917	Bolsheviks seize power.
1918	Czar and family are murdered.
1922	Lenin announces creation of the Union of Soviet Socialist Republics (USSR).
1922	Stalin takes control.
1941-1945	Adolph Hitler invades Russia, 25,000,000 citizens killed.
1945	Germany is defeated.
1953	Stalin dies; Nikita Khrushchev takes control.
1964-1982	Leonid Brezhnev takes control; Cold War.
1985	Mikhail Gorbachev takes control.
1991	Gorbachev overthrown; Boris Yeltsin forms Commonwealth of Independent States.
1996	Yeltsin victorious in presidential election.
1997	Yeltsin and U.S. President Bill Clinton sign mutual cooperation treaty.
1996-1998	Economic crisis.
2000	Vladimir Putin elected president.

Sources

CHAPTER ONE: A German Princess

p. 15, "rarely is music anything . . ." Henri Troyat, *Catherine the Great* (New York: E. P. Dutton, 1980), 4.

p. 23, "No one could see Elizabeth . . ." Joan Haslip, *Catherine the Great* (New York: G. P. Putnam's Sons, 1977), 29.

p. 25, "I cared very little . . ." Haslip, *Catherine*, 30.

p. 26, "There was no fundamental . . ." Ibid., 36.

CHAPTER TWO: Marriage and a New Life

p. 28, "I had become thin . . ." Catherine II, *The Memoirs of Catherine the Great* (New York: The Macmillan Co., 1955), 65.

p. 28, "an uneducated lout" Haslip, *Catherine*, 41.

p. 29, "My heart boded no good." Troyat, *Catherine*, 30.

p. 33, "You think of nothing . . ." Ibid, 39.

p. 34, "he had become quite horrid . . ." Catherine II, *Memoirs*, 87.

p. 34, "I evinced great respect . . ." Ibid, *Memoirs*, 89.

p. 36, "I would have been ready . . ." Ibid, *Memoirs*, 101.

p, 37, "by her sensible behavior . . ." Zoé Oldenbourgh, *Catherine the Great* (New York: Random House, Inc., 1965), 111.

CHAPTER THREE: An Apprentice to the Throne

p. 40, "it was not for me . . ." Troyat, *Catherine*, 37.

p. 40, "I was improving in looks . . ." Catherine II, *Memoirs*, 133.

p. 42, "I held firm . . ." Ibid, 200.

p. 43, "I could not get it out . . ." Troyat, *Catherine*, 77.

p. 45, "a very meager necklace . . ." Haslip, *Catherine*, 66.

p. 45, "I resolved to make . . ." Troyat, *Catherine*, 81.

p. 45, "I walked with my . . ." Ibid., 81.

p. 48, "my heart cannot be content . . ." Ibid., 81.

p. 49, "the Grand Duke . . ." Ibid., 89.

p. 50, "It is my dream . . ." Haslip, *Catherine*, 83.

p. 51, "I have already laid . . ." Ibid., 77.

p. 52, "I regarded his plan . . ." Troyat, *Catherine*, 92.

p. 55, "last drop of German blood . . ." Haslip, *Catherine*, 146.

CHAPTER FOUR: Czarina Catherine II

p. 60, "no one is more assiduous . . ." Haslip, *Catherine*, 117.

p. 66, "exposed to extreme danger . . ." Ibid., 129.

p. 66, "the glory of Russia . . ." Ibid., 130.

p. 66, "Long live our Little Mother . . ." Ibid., 128.

p. 70, "her figure is noble . . ." Alexander, *Catherine*, 5.

p. 71, "My reputation is ruined . . ." Troyat, p. 155.

p. 74, "To join the Caspian Sea . . ." Oldenbourgh, *Catherine*, 256.

CHAPTER FIVE: Building an Empire

p. 75, "A man's dress . . ." John Alexander, *Catherine the Great: Life and Legend* (New York: Oxford Univ. Press, 1989), 65.

p. 78, "Our Grandfather Emperor . . ." Ibid., 78.

p. 79, "One should do good . . ." Catherine II, *Memoirs*, 4.

p. 83, "I cannot live one hour . . ." Haslip, *Catherine*, 148.

p. 85, "stammering and unintelligible . . ." Ibid., 151.

p. 85, "murderess, assassin, usurper . . ." Haslip, *Catherine*, 190.

p. 86, "Her conversation is brilliant . . ." Alexander, *Catherine*, 100.

p. 87, "She has a fine mouth . . ." Troyat, *Catherine*, 158.

p. 89, "I will make a king . . ." Ibid., 162.

CHAPTER SIX: War

p. 95, "They say that the earth . . ." Alexander, *Catherine*, 133.

p. 97-98, "in order to reestablish . . ." Troyat, *Catherine*, 195.

p. 102, "You will no longer work . . ." Oldenbourg, *Catherine*, 299.

p. 103, "I have been obliged . . ." Haslip, *Catherine*, 211.

p. 105, "at the end of each one . . ." Ibid., 190.

p. 105, "every Russian peasant . . ." Ibid., 191.

p. 108, "They love each other . . ." Ibid., 237.

CHAPTER SEVEN: Enlightened Despot

p. 111,"The princess' religious . . ." Haslip, *Catherine*, 248.

p. 112, "magnificence and good taste . . ." Ibid., 258.

p. 122, "man of gold" Ibid., 288.

p. 122, "I have found a friend . . ." Ibid., 304.

CHAPTER EIGHT: Potemkin Village

p. 126, "to see the conqueror . . ." Haslip, *Catherine*, 304.

p. 126, "the pleasantest company . . ." Ibid., 304.

p. 131, "in two weeks . . ." Alexander, *Catherine*, 263.

p. 138, "I'm dying . . ." Haslip, *Catherine*, 354.

p. 138, "Whom shall I rely . . ." Ibid., 354.

CHAPTER NINE: The Future is the Past

p. 142, "the troops of her imperial . . ." Haslip, *Catherine*, 356.

p. 146, "*Catherine le Grand* . . ." Troyat, *Catherine*, 348.

p. 146-147, "Here lies Catherine the Second . . ." Ibid., 305.

Bibliography

Alexander, John. *Catherine the Great: Life and Legend.* New York: Oxford University Press, 1989.

Catherine II. *The Memoirs of Catherine the Great.* New York: The Macmillan Company, 1955.

Haslip, Joan. *Catherine the Great.* New York: G.P. Putnam's Sons, 1977.

Kochan, Miriam. *Catherine the Great.* England: Wayland Publishers Ltd, 1976.

Madariaga, Isabel. *Catherine the Great: A Short History.* New Haven: Yale University Press, 1990.

Oldenbourg, Zoé *Catherine the Great.* New York: Random House, Inc., 1965.

Segal, Harold B. (ed) vols I and II. *Literature of Eighteenth-Century Russia.* New York: E. P. Dutton & Co., Inc., 1967.

Troyat, Henri (translated by Joan Pinkham). *Catherine the Great.* New York: E. P. Dutton, 1977.

Web sites

Catherine II (the Great) links
http://wasa.uk.net/history/links/Russia/Catherine_ll.html

A Chronology of Russian History
www.departmentc.bucknell.edu/russian/history.html

History House, an online history magazine
www.historyhouse.com

Manifesto of Czarina Catherine II
http://members.aol.com/jktsn/manifest/htm

Modern History Sourcebook: Catherine the Great
http://www.fordham.edu/halsall/mod/18catherine.html

Index